BEING BROUGHT
FROM AFRICA TO AMERICA

THE BEST OF PHILLIS WHEATLEY

By

PHILLIS WHEATLEY

Read & Co.

Copyright © 2020 Ragged Hand

This edition is published by Ragged Hand,
an imprint of Read & Co.

British Library Cataloguing-in-Publication Data
A catalogue record for this book is available
from the British Library.

Read & Co. is part of Read Books Ltd.
For more information visit
www.readandcobooks.co.uk

CONTENTS

Phillis Wheatley

A poet, born in Africa about 1753; died in Boston, Mass., 5 Dec., 1784. She was brought here from Africa in 1761, and her only recollection of her early life was that of her heathen mother worshipping the sun at its rising.

She was bought from the slave-market by John Wheatley, of Boston, and soon developed remarkable acquisitive faculties. She became a member of his family and was educated by his daughters. In sixteen months from her arrival she could read English fluently, soon learned to write, and also studied Latin. She visited England in 1774, where she was cordially received, and after her return to Boston she corresponded with the Countess of Huntingdon, the Earl of Dartmouth, Rev. George Whitefield, and others, and wrote many poems to her friends. She addressed some lines and a letter to Gen. Washington on 26 Oct., 1775, which were afterward published in the *Pennsylvania Magazine, or American Monthly Museum*, for April, 1776. In a reply, under date of 2 Feb., 1776, Gen. Washington writes: "I thank you most sincerely for your polite notice of me in the elegant lines you inclosed; and, however undeserving I may be of such encomium and panegyric, the style and manner exhibit a striking proof of your poetical talents; in honor of which, and as a tribute justly due to you, I would have published the poem had I not been apprehensive that, while I only meant to give the world this new instance of your genius, I might have incurred the imputation of vanity. This, and nothing else, determined me not to give it place in the public prints. If you should ever come to Cambridge, or near headquarters. I shall be happy to see a person so favored by the muses, and to whom Nature has been so liberal and beneficent in her dispensations."

A few days before the British evacuated Boston she visited the

Revolutionary camp and was received with marked attention by Washington and his officers. Thomas Jefferson said that her verses were beneath criticism.

In 1775 the Wheatley family was broken up by death, and, after attempting and failing to support herself, she married in 1778 a colored man named Peters, who, according to different accounts, was a grocer, lawyer, or barber. This marriage proved unhappy, and Peters became reduced in circumstances. During the Revolution they resided in Wilmington, Del., and they afterward returned to Boston, where they lived in wretched poverty. Among the attentions that she received in London was a gift from the lord mayor of a copy of *Paradise Lost*, which was sold after her death, and is now in the library of Harvard. Her publications are *An Elegiac Poem on the Death of George Whitefield, Chaplain to the Countess of Huntingdon* (Boston, 1770); *Poems on Various Subjects, Religious and Moral, by Phillis Wheatley, Negro Servant to Mr. John Wheatley, of Boston*, to certify which an attestation was addressed to the public and signed by Gov. Thomas Hutchinson, John Hancock, Rev. Samuel Mather, John Wheatley, Andrew Eliot, and others (London, 1773; 3d ed., Albany, 1793; republished as *The Negro Equalled by Few Europeans*, 2 vols., Philadelphia, 1801; 2d ed., Walpole, N. H., 1802; 3d ed., with a memoir, Boston, 1834); and *Elegy Sacred to the Memory of Dr. Samuel Cooper* (1784). The *Letters of Phillis Wheatley* were printed privately by Charles Deane from the *Proceedings of the Massachusetts Historical Society* (Boston, 1864).

A BIOGRAPHY FROM
Appletons' Cyclopædia of American Biography, 1889.

PHILLIS WHEATLEY

By Benjamin Brawley

Phillis Wheatley was born very probably in 1753. The poem on Whitefield published in 1770 said on the title-page that she was seventeen years old. When she came to Boston she was shedding her front teeth. Her memory of her childhood in Africa was always vague. She knew only that her mother *poured out water before the rising sun.* This was probably a rite of heathen worship.

Mrs. Wheatley was a woman of unusual refinement. Her home was well known to the people of fashion and culture in Boston, and King Street in which she lived was then as noted for its residences as it is now, under the name of State Street, famous for its commercial and banking houses. When Phillis entered the Wheatley home the family consisted of four persons, Mr. and Mrs. Wheatley, their son Nathaniel, and their daughter Mary. Nathaniel and Mary were twins, born May 4, 1743. Mrs. Wheatley was also the mother of three other children, Sarah, John, and Susannah; but all of these died in early youth. Mary Wheatley, accordingly, was the only daughter of the family that Phillis knew to any extent, and she was eighteen years old when her mother brought the child to the house, that is, just a little more than ten years older than Phillis.

In her new home the girl showed signs of remarkable talent. Her childish desire for expression found an outlet in the figures which she drew with charcoal or chalk on the walls of the house. Mrs. Wheatley and her daughter became so interested in the ease with which she assimilated knowledge that they began to teach her. Within sixteen months from the time of her arrival in Boston Phillis was able to read fluently the most difficult parts of the Bible. From the first her mistress strove to cultivate in every possible way her naturally pious disposition, and diligently gave her instruction in the Scriptures and in morals. In course of time, thanks especially to the teaching of Mary Wheatley, the learning of the young student came to consist of a little astronomy, some ancient and modern geography, a little ancient history, a fair knowledge of the Bible, and a thoroughly appreciative acquaintance with the most important Latin classics, especially the works of Virgil and Ovid. She was proud of the fact that Terence was at least of African birth.

She became proficient in grammar, developing a conception of style from practice rather than from theory. Pope's translation of Homer was her favorite English classic. If in the light of twentieth century opportunity and methods these attainments seem in no wise remarkable, one must remember the disadvantages under which not only Phillis Wheatley, but all the women of her time, labored; and recall that in any case her attainments would have marked her as one of the most highly educated young women in Boston.

While Phillis was trying to make the most of her time with her studies, she was also seeking to develop herself in other ways. She had not been studying long before she began to feel that she too would like to make verses.

Alexander Pope was still an important force in English literature, and the young student became his ready pupil. She was about fourteen years old when she seriously began to cultivate her poetic talent; and one of the very earliest, and from every standpoint one of the most interesting of her efforts is the pathetic little juvenile poem, "On Being Brought from Africa to America:"

'Twas mercy brought me from my pagan land,
Taught my benighted soul to understand
That there's a God—that there's a Saviour too:
Once I redemption neither sought nor knew.
Some view our sable race with scornful eye—
"Their colour is a diabolic dye."
Remember, Christians, Negroes black as Cain
May be refined, and join th' angelic train.

Meanwhile, the life of Phillis was altogether different from that of the other slaves of the household. No hard labor was required of her, though she did the lighter work, such as dusting a room or polishing a table. Gradually she came to be regarded as a daughter and companion rather than as a slave. As she wrote poetry, more and more she proved to have a talent for writing occasional verse. Whenever any unusual event, such as a death, occurred in any family of the circle of Mrs. Wheatley's acquaintance, she would write lines on the same. She thus came to be regarded as "a kind of poet-laureate in the domestic circles of Boston." She was frequently invited to the homes of people to whom Mrs. Wheatley had introduced her, and was regarded with peculiar interest and esteem, on account both of her singular position and her lovable nature. In her own room at home Phillis was specially permitted to have heat and a light, because her constitution was delicate, and in order that she might write down her thoughts as they came to her, rather than trust them to her fickle memory.

Such for some years was the course of the life of Phillis Wheatley. The year 1770 saw the earliest publication of one of her poems. On the first printed page of this edition one might read the following announcement: "A Poem, By Phillis, a Negro Girl, in Boston, On the Death of the Reverend George Whitefield." In the middle of the page is a quaint representation of the dead man in his coffin, on the top of which one might with difficulty decipher, "G. W. Ob. 30 Sept. 1770, Aet. 56."

The poem is addressed to the Countess of Huntingdon, whom Whitefield had served as chaplain, and to the orphan children of Georgia whom he had befriended. It takes up in the original less than four pages of large print. It was revised for the 1773 edition of the poems.

In 1771 the first real sorrow of Phillis Wheatley came to her. On January 31st Mary Wheatley left the old home to become the wife of Rev. John Lathrop, pastor of the Second Church in Boston. This year is important for another event. On August 18th "Phillis, the servant of Mr. Wheatley," became a communicant of the Old South Meeting House in Boston. We are informed that "her membership in Old South was an exception to the rule that slaves were not baptized into the church." At that time the church was without a regular minister, though it had lately received the excellent teaching of the Rev. Dr. Joseph Sewell.

This was a troublous time in the history of Boston. Already the storm of the Revolution was gathering. The period was one of vexation on the part of the slaves and their masters as well as on that of the colonies and England. The argument on the side of the slaves was that, as the colonies were still English territory, they were technically free, Lord Mansfield having handed down the decision in 1772 that as soon as a slave touched the soil of England he became free. Certainly Phillis must have been a girl of unusual tact to be able under such conditions to hold so securely the esteem and affection of her many friends.

About this time, as we learn from her correspondence, her health began to fail. Almost all of her letters that are preserved were written to Obour Tanner, a friend living in Newport, R. I. Just when the two young women became acquainted is not known. Obour Tanner survived until the fourth decade of the next century. It was to her, then, still a young woman, that on July 19, 1772, Phillis wrote from Boston as follows:

My Dear Friend,—

I received your kind epistle a few days ago; much disappointed to hear that you had not received my answer to your first letter. I have been in a very poor state of health all the past winter and spring, and now reside in the country for the benefit of its more wholesome air. I came to town this morning to spend the Sabbath with my master and mistress. Let me be interested in your prayers that God will bless to me the means used for my recovery, if agreeable to his holy will.

By the spring of 1773 the condition of the health of Phillis was such as to give her friends much concern. The family physician advised that she try the air of the sea. As Nathaniel Wheatley was just then going to England, it was decided that she should accompany him. The two sailed in May. The poem, "A Farewell to America," is dated May 7, 1773. It was addressed to "S. W.," that is, Mrs. Wheatley. Before she left America, Phillis was formally manumitted.

The poem on Whitefield served well as an introduction to the Countess of Huntingdon. Through the influence of this noblewoman Phillis met other ladies, and for the summer the child of the wilderness was the pet of the society people of England. Now it was that a peculiar gift of Phillis Wheatley shone to advantage.

To the recommendations of a strange history, ability to write verses, and the influence of kind friends, she added the accomplishment of brilliant conversation. Presents were showered upon her. One that has been preserved is a copy of the magnificent 1770 Glasgow folio edition of "Paradise Lost," given to her by Brook Watson, Lord Mayor of London. This book is now in the library of Harvard University. At the top of one of the first pages, in the handwriting of Phillis Wheatley, are these words:

"Mr. Brook Watson to Phillis Wheatley, London, July, 1773."

At the bottom of the same page, in the handwriting of another, are these words:

"This book was given by Brook Watson formerly Lord Mayor of London to Phillis Wheatley & after her death was sold in payment of her husband's debts. It is now presented to the Library of Harvard University at Cambridge, by Dudley L. Pickman of Salem. March, 1824."

Phillis had not arrived in England at the most fashionable season, however. The ladies of the circle of the Countess of Huntingdon desired that she remain long enough to be presented at the court of George III. An accident—the illness of Mrs. Wheatley—prevented the introduction. This lady longed for the presence of her old companion, and Phillis could not be persuaded to delay her return. Before she went back to Boston, however, arrangements were made for the publication of her volume, "Poems on Various Subjects, Religious and Moral," of which more must be said. While the book does not of course contain the later scattered poems, it is the only collection ever brought together by Phillis Wheatley, and the book by which she is known.

The visit to England marked the highest point in the career of the young author. Her piety and faith were now to be put to their severest test, and her noble bearing under hardship and disaster must forever speak to her credit. In much of the sorrow that came to her she was not alone, for the period of the Revolution was one of general distress.

Phillis remained in England barely four months. In October she was back in Boston. That she was little improved may be seen from the letter to Obour Tanner, bearing date the 30th of this month:

14

I hear of your welfare with pleasure; but this acquaints you that I am at present indisposed by a cold, and since my arrival have been visited by the asthma.

A postscript to this letter reads:

> The young man by whom this is handed to you seems to be a very clever man, knows you very well, and is very complaisant and agreeable.

The "young man" was John Peters, afterwards to be her husband.

A great sorrow came to Phillis in the death on March 3, 1774, of her best friend, Mrs. Wheatley, then in her sixty-fifth year. How she felt about this event is best set forth in her own words in a letter addressed to Obour Tanner at Newport under date March 21, 1774:

DEAR OBOUR,—

I received your obliging letter enclosed in your Reverend Pastor's and handed me by his son. I have lately met with a great trial in the death of my mistress; let us imagine the loss of a parent, sister or brother, the tenderness of all were united in her. I was a poor little outcast and a stranger when she took me in; not only into her house, but I presently became a sharer in her most tender affections. I was treated by her more like her child than her servant; no opportunity was left unimproved of giving me the best of advice; but in terms how tender! how engaging! This I hope ever to keep in remembrance. Her exemplary life was a greater monitor than all her precepts and instructions; thus we may observe of how much greater force example is than instruction. To alleviate our sorrows we had the satisfaction to see her depart in inexpressible raptures, earnest longings, and impatient thirstings for the *upper* courts of the Lord. Do, my dear friend, remember me and this family in your closet, that

15

this afflicting dispensation may be sanctified to us. I am very sorry to hear that you are indisposed, but hope this will find you in better health. I have been unwell the greater part of the winter, but am much better as the spring approaches. Pray excuse my not writing you so long before, for I have been so busy lately that I could not find leisure. I shall send the 5 books you wrote for, the first convenient opportunity; if you want more they shall be ready for you. I am very affectionately your friend,

PHILLIS WHEATLEY.

After the death of Mrs. Wheatley Phillis seems not to have lived regularly at the old home; at least one of her letters written in 1775 was sent from Providence. For Mr. Wheatley the house must have been a sad one; his daughter was married and living in her own home, his son was living abroad, and his wife was dead. It was in this darkening period of her life, however, that a very pleasant experience came to Phillis Wheatley. This was her reception at the hands of George Washington. In 1775, while the siege of Boston was in progress, she wrote a letter to the distinguished soldier, enclosing a complimentary poem. Washington later replied as follows:

Cambridge, Feb. 2, 1776.

MISS PHILLIS,—

Your favor of the 26th of October did not reach my hand till the middle of December. Time enough, you say, to have given an answer ere this. Granted. But a variety of important occurrences continually interposing to distract the mind and to withdraw the attention, I hope, will apologize for the delay and plead my excuse for the seeming, but not real neglect. I thank you most sincerely for your polite notice of me, in the elegant lines you enclosed, and however undeserving I may be of such encomium

16

and panegyric, the style and manner exhibit a striking proof of your poetical talents, in honor of which, and as a tribute justly due to you, I would have published the poem, had I not been apprehensive that while I only meant to give the world this new instance of your genius, I might have incurred the imputation of vanity. This and nothing else determined me not to give it place in the public prints. If you should ever come to Cambridge or near headquarters, I shall be happy to see a person so favored by the muses, and to whom Nature has been so liberal and beneficent in her dispensations.

I am, with great respect,
Your obedient humble servant,

GEORGE WASHINGTON.

Not long afterwards Phillis accepted the invitation of the General and was received in Cambridge with marked courtesy by Washington and his officers.

The Wheatley home was finally broken up by the death of Mr. John Wheatley, March 12, 1778, at the age of seventy-two. After this event Phillis lived for a short time with a friend of Mrs. Wheatley, and then took an apartment and lived by herself. By April she had yielded to the blandishments of John Peters sufficiently to be persuaded to become his wife. This man is variously reported to have been a baker, a barber, a grocer, a doctor, and a lawyer. With all of these professions and occupations, however, he seems not to have possessed the ability to make a living. He wore a wig, sported a cane, and generally felt himself superior to labor. Bereft of old friends as she was, however, sick and lonely, it is not surprising that when love and care seemed thus to present themselves the heart of the woman yielded. It was not long before she realized that she was married to a ne'er-do-well at a time when even an industrious man found it hard to make a living. The course of the Revolutionary War made it more and more difficult for people to secure the bare necessaries of life, and the horrors of Valley Forge were but an aggravation of the general distress. The year was further made memorable by the death of Mary Wheatley, Mrs. Lathrop, on the 24th of September.

When Boston fell into the hands of the British, the inhabitants fled in all directions. Mrs. Peters accompanied her husband to Wilmington, Mass., where she suffered much from poverty. After the evacuation of Boston by the British troops, she returned thither. A niece of Mrs. Wheatley, whose son had been slain in battle, received her under her own roof. This woman was a widow, was not wealthy, and kept a little school in order to support herself. Mrs. Peters and the two children whose mother she had become remained with her for six weeks. Then Peters came for his wife, having provided an apartment for her. Just before her departure for Wilmington, Mrs. Peters entrusted her papers to a daughter of the lady who received her on her return from that place. After her death these were demanded by Peters as the property of his wife. They were of course promptly given to him. Some years afterwards he returned to the South, and nothing is known of what became of the manuscripts.

The conduct of her husband estranged Mrs. Peters from her old acquaintances, and her pride kept her from informing them of her distress. After the war, however, one of Mrs. Wheatley's relatives hunted her out and found that her two children were dead, and that a third that had been born was sick. This seems to have been in the winter of 1783-84. Nathaniel Wheatley, who had been living in London, died in the summer of 1783. In 1784 John Peters suffered imprisonment in jail. After his liberation he worked as a journeyman baker, later attempted to practice law, and finally pretended to be a physician. His wife, meanwhile, earned her board by drudgery in a cheap lodging-house on the west side of the town. Her disease made rapid progress, and she died December 5, 1784. Her last baby died and was buried with her. No one of her old acquaintances seems to have known of her death. On the Thursday after this event, however, the following notice appeared in the *Independent Chronicle*:

Last Lord's Day, died Mrs. Phillis Peters (formerly Phillis Wheatley), aged thirty-one, known to the world by her celebrated miscellaneous poems. Her funeral is to be this afternoon, at four o'clock, from the house lately improved by Mr. Todd, nearly opposite Dr. Bulfinch's at West Boston, where her friends and acquaintances are desired to attend.

The house referred to was situated on or near the present site of the Revere House in Bowdoin Square. The exact site of the grave of Phillis Wheatley is not known.

At the time when she was most talked about, Phillis Wheatley was regarded as a prodigy, appearing as she did at a time when the achievement of the Negro in literature and art was still negligible. Her vogue, however, was more than temporary, and the 1793, 1802, and 1816 editions of her poems found ready sale. In the early years of the last century her verses were frequently to be found in school readers. From the first, however, there were those who discounted her poetry. Thomas Jefferson, for instance, said that it was beneath the dignity of criticism. If after 1816 interest in her work declined, it was greatly revived at the time of the anti-slavery agitation, when anything indicating unusual capacity on the part of the Negro was received with eagerness. When Margaretta Matilda Odell of Jamaica Plain, a descendant of the Wheatley family, republished the poems with a memoir in 1834, there was such a demand for the book that two more editions were called for within the next three years. For a variety of reasons, especially an increasing race-consciousness on the part of the Negro, interest in her work has greatly increased within the last decade, and as copies of early editions had within recent years become so rare as to be practically inaccessible, the reprint in 1909 of the volume of 1773 by the A. M. E. Book Concern in Philadelphia was especially welcome.

Only two poems written by Phillis Wheatley after her marriage are in existence. These are "Liberty and Peace," and

"An Elegy Sacred to the Memory of Dr. Samuel Cooper."

The little octavo volume of 124 pages contains 39 poems. One of these, however, must be excluded from the enumeration, as it is simply "A Rebus by I. B.," which serves as the occasion of Phillis Wheatley's poem, the answer to it. Fourteen of the poems are elegiac, and at least six others are occasional. Two are paraphrases from the Bible. We are thus left with sixteen poems to represent the best that Phillis Wheatley had produced by the time she was twenty years old. One of the longest of these is "Niobe in Distress for Her Children Slain by Apollo, from Ovid's Metamorphoses, Book VI, and from a View of the Painting of Mr. Richard Wilson." This poem contains two interesting examples of personification (neither of which seems to be drawn from Ovid), "fate portentous whistling in the air," and "the feather'd vengeance quiv'ring in his hands," though the point might easily be made that these are little more than a part of the pseudo-classic tradition. The poem, "To S. M., a Young African Painter, on seeing his works," was addressed to Scipio Moorhead, a young man who exhibited some talent for drawing and who was a servant of the Rev. John Moorhead of Boston. From the poem we should infer that one of his subjects was the story of Damon and Pythias. Of prime importance are the two or three poems of autobiographical interest. We have already remarked "On Being Brought from Africa to America." In the lines addressed to William, Earl of Dartmouth, the young woman spoke again from her personal experience. Important also in this connection is the poem "On Virtue," with its plea:

> Attend me, Virtue, thro' my youthful years!
> O leave me not to the false joys of time!
> But guide my steps to endless life and bliss.

One would suppose that Phillis Wheatley would make of "An Hymn to Humanity" a fairly strong piece of work. It is typical of the restraint under which she labored that this is one of the most conventional things in the volume.

All critics agree, however, that the strongest lines in the book are those entitled "On Imagination." This effort is more sustained than the others, and it is the leading poem that Edmund Clarence Stedman chose to represent Phillis Wheatley in his "Library of American Literature." The following lines are representative of its quality:

> Imagination! Who can sing thy force?
> Or who describe the swiftness of thy course?
> Soaring through air to find the bright abode,
> Th' empyreal palace of the thundering God,
> We on thy pinions can surpass the wind,
> And leave the rolling universe behind:
> From star to star the mental optics rove,
> Measure the skies, and range the realms above;
> There in one view we grasp the mighty whole,
> Or with new worlds amaze th' unbounded soul.

Hardly beyond this is "Liberty and Peace," the best example of the later verse. The poem is too long for inclusion here, but may be found in Duyckinck's "Cyclopedia of American Literature," and Heartman and Schomburg's collected edition of the Poems and Letters.

It is unfortunate that, imitating Pope, Phillis Wheatley more than once fell into his pitfalls. Her diction—"fleecy care," "vital breath," "feather'd race"—is distinctly pseudo-classic. The construction is not always clear; for instance, in the poem, "To Mæcenas," there are three distinct references to Virgil, when grammatically the poetess seems to be speaking of three different men. Then, of course, any young writer working under the influence of Pope and his school would feel a sense of repression. If Phillis Wheatley had come on the scene forty years later, when the romantic writers had given a new tone to English poetry, she would undoubtedly have been much greater.

Even as it was, however, she made her mark, and her place in the history of American literature, though not a large one, is secure.

Hers was a great soul. Her ambition knew no bounds, her thirst for knowledge was insatiable, and she triumphed over the most adverse circumstances. A child of the wilderness and a slave, by her grace and culture she satisfied the conventionalities of Boston and of England. Her brilliant conversation was equaled only by her modest demeanor. Everything about her was refined. More and more as one studies her life he becomes aware of her sterling Christian character. In a dark day she caught a glimpse of the eternal light, and it was meet that the first Negro woman in American literature should be one of unerring piety and the highest of literary ideals.

A Chapter from
The Negro in Literature and Art in the United States, 1910

BEING BROUGHT
FROM AFRICA TO AMERICA

THE BEST OF PHILLIS WHEATLEY

TO MAECENAS

MAECENAS, you, beneath the myrtle shade,
Read o'er what poets sung, and shepherds play'd.
What felt those poets but you feel the same?
Does not your soul possess the sacred flame?
Their noble strains your equal genius shares
In softer language, and diviner airs.
   While Homer paints, lo! circumfus'd in air,
Celestial Gods in mortal forms appear;
Swift as they move hear each recess rebound,
Heav'n quakes, earth trembles, and the shores resound.
Great Sire of verse, before my mortal eyes,
The lightnings blaze across the vaulted skies,
And, as the thunder shakes the heav'nly plains,
A deep felt horror thrills through all my veins.
When gentler strains demand thy graceful song,
The length'ning line moves languishing along.
When great Patroclus courts Achilles' aid,
The grateful tribute of my tears is paid;
Prone on the shore he feels the pangs of love,
And stern Pelides tend'rest passions move.
   Great Maro's strain in heav'nly numbers flows,
The Nine inspire, and all the bosom glows.
O could I rival thine and Virgil's page,
Or claim the Muses with the Mantuan Sage;
Soon the same beauties should my mind adorn,
And the same ardors in my soul should burn:
Then should my song in bolder notes arise,
And all my numbers pleasingly surprise;
But here I sit, and mourn a grov'ling mind,

That fain would mount, and ride upon the wind.
   Not you, my friend, these plaintive strains become,
Not you, whose bosom is the Muses home;
When they from tow'ring Helicon retire,
They fan in you the bright immortal fire,
But I less happy, cannot raise the song,
The fault'ring music dies upon my tongue.
   The happier Terence[1] all the choir inspir'd,
His soul replenish'd, and his bosom fir'd;
But say, ye Muses, why this partial grace,
To one alone of Afric's sable race;
From age to age transmitting thus his name
With the finest glory in the rolls of fame?
   Thy virtues, great Maecenas! shall be sung
In praise of him, from whom those virtues sprung:
While blooming wreaths around thy temples spread,
I'll snatch a laurel from thine honour'd head,
While you indulgent smile upon the deed.
   As long as Thames in streams majestic flows,
Or Naiads in their oozy beds repose
While Phoebus reigns above the starry train
While bright Aurora purples o'er the main,
So long, great Sir, the muse thy praise shall sing,
So long thy praise shal' make Parnassus ring:
Then grant, Maecenas, thy paternal rays,
Hear me propitious, and defend my lays.

---

1 He was an African by birth.

ON VIRTUE

O Thou bright jewel in my aim I strive
To comprehend thee. Thine own words declare
Wisdom is higher than a fool can reach.
I cease to wonder, and no more attempt
Thine height t' explore, or fathom thy profound.
But, O my soul, sink not into despair,
Virtue is near thee, and with gentle hand
Would now embrace thee, hovers o'er thine head.
Fain would the heav'n-born soul with her converse,
Then seek, then court her for her promis'd bliss.
   Auspicious queen, thine heav'nly pinions spread,
And lead celestial Chastity along;
Lo! now her sacred retinue descends,
Array'd in glory from the orbs above.
Attend me, Virtue, thro' my youthful years!
O leave me not to the false joys of time!
But guide my steps to endless life and bliss.
Greatness, or Goodness, say what I shall call thee,
To give me an higher appellation still,
Teach me a better strain, a nobler lay,
O thou, enthron'd with Cherubs in the realms of day.

TO THE
UNIVERSITY OF CAMBRIDGE

IN NEW-ENGLAND

WHILE an intrinsic ardor prompts to write,
The muses promise to assist my pen;
'Twas not long since I left my native shore
The land of errors, and Egyptian gloom:
Father of mercy, 'twas thy gracious hand
Brought me in safety from those dark abodes.
  Students, to you 'tis giv'n to scan the heights
Above, to traverse the ethereal space,
And mark the systems of revolving worlds.
Still more, ye sons of science ye receive
The blissful news by messengers from heav'n,
How Jesus' blood for your redemption flows.
See him with hands out-stretcht upon the cross;
Immense compassion in his bosom glows;
He hears revilers, nor resents their scorn:
What matchless mercy in the Son of God!
When the whole human race by sin had fall'n,
He deign'd to die that they might rise again,
And share with him in the sublimest skies,
Life without death, and glory without end.
  Improve your privileges while they stay,
Ye pupils, and each hour redeem, that bears
Or good or bad report of you to heav'n.
Let sin, that baneful evil to the soul,
By you be shun'd, nor once remit your guard;

Suppress the deadly serpent in its egg.
Ye blooming plants of human race divine,
An Ethiop tells you 'tis your greatest foe;
Its transient sweetness turns to endless pain,
And in immense perdition sinks the soul.

TO THE KING'S MOST EXCELLENT MAJESTY

1768

YOUR subjects hope, dread Sire—
The crown upon your brows may flourish long,
And that your arm may in your God be strong!
O may your sceptre num'rous nations sway,
And all with love and readiness obey!
    But how shall we the British king reward!
Rule thou in peace, our father, and our lord!
Midst the remembrance of thy favours past,
The meanest peasants most admire the last[2]
May George, beloved by all the nations round,
Live with heav'ns choicest constant blessings crown'd!
Great God, direct, and guard him from on high,
And from his head let ev'ry evil fly!
And may each clime with equal gladness see
A monarch's smile can set his subjects free!

---

2 The Repeal of the Stamp Act.

ON BEING BROUGHT
FROM AFRICA TO AMERICA

———————————

'Twas mercy brought me from my Pagan land,
Taught my benighted soul to understand
That there's a God, that there's a Saviour too:
Once I redemption neither fought nor knew,
Some view our sable race with scornful eye,
"Their colour is a diabolic die."
Remember, Christians, Negroes, black as Cain,
May be refin'd, and join th' angelic train.

ON THE DEATH OF
THE REV. DR. SEWELL

1769

ERE yet the morn its lovely blushes spread,
See Sewell number'd with the happy dead.
Hail, holy man, arriv'd th' immortal shore,
Though we shall hear thy warning voice no more.
Come, let us all behold with wishful eyes
The saint ascending to his native skies;
From hence the prophet wing'd his rapt'rous way
To the blest mansions in eternal day.
Then begging for the Spirit of our God,
And panting eager for the same abode,
Come, let us all with the same vigour rise,
And take a prospect of the blissful skies;
While on our minds Christ's image is imprest,
And the dear Saviour glows in ev'ry breast.
Thrice happy saint! to find thy heav'n at last,
What compensation for the evils past!
   Great God, incomprehensible, unknown
By sense, we bow at thine exalted throne.
O, while we beg thine excellence to feel,
Thy sacred Spirit to our hearts reveal,
And give us of that mercy to partake,
Which thou hast promis'd for the Saviour's sake!
   "Sewell is dead." Swift-pinion'd Fame thus cry'd.
"Is Sewell dead," my trembling tongue reply'd,
O what a blessing in his flight deny'd!

How oft for us the holy prophet pray'd!
How oft to us the Word of Life convey'd!
By duty urg'd my mournful verse to close,
I for his tomb this epitaph compose.
  "Lo, here a man, redeem'd by Jesus's blood,
"A sinner once, but now a saint with God;
"Behold ye rich, ye poor, ye fools, ye wise,
"Not let his monument your heart surprise;
"Twill tell you what this holy man has done,
"Which gives him brighter lustre than the sun.
"Listen, ye happy, from your seats above.
"I speak sincerely, while I speak and love,
"He fought the paths of piety and truth,
"By these made happy from his early youth;
"In blooming years that grace divine he felt,
"Which rescues sinners from the chains of guilt.
"Mourn him, ye indigent, whom he has fed,
"And henceforth seek, like him, for living bread;
"Ev'n Christ, the bread descending from above,
"And ask an int'rest in his saving love.
"Mourn him, ye youth, to whom he oft has told
"God's gracious wonders from the times of old.
"I too have cause this mighty loss to mourn,
"For he my monitor will not return.
"O when shall we to his blest state arrive?
"When the same graces in our bosoms thrive."

ON THE DEATH OF THE
REV. MR. GEORGE WHITEFIELD

1770

HAIL, happy saint, on thine immortal throne,
Possest of glory, life, and bliss unknown;
We hear no more the music of thy tongue,
Thy wonted auditories cease to throng.
Thy sermons in unequall'd accents flow'd,
And ev'ry bosom with devotion glow'd;
Thou didst in strains of eloquence refin'd
Inflame the heart, and captivate the mind.
Unhappy we the setting sun deplore,
So glorious once, but ah! it shines no more.
   Behold the prophet in his tow'ring flight!
He leaves the earth for heav'n's unmeasur'd height,
And worlds unknown receive him from our sight.
There Whitefield wings with rapid course his way,
And sails to Zion through vast seas of day.
Thy pray'rs, great saint, and thine incessant cries
Have pierc'd the bosom of thy native skies.
Thou moon hast seen, and all the stars of light,
How he has wrestled with his God by night.
He pray'd that grace in ev'ry heart might dwell,
He long'd to see America excell;
He charg'd its youth that ev'ry grace divine
Should with full lustre in their conduct shine;
That Saviour, which his soul did first receive,
The greatest gift that ev'n a God can give,

He freely offer'd to the num'rous throng,
That on his lips with list'ning pleasure hung.
   "Take him, ye wretched, for your only good,
"Take him ye starving sinners, for your food;
"Ye thirsty, come to this life-giving stream,
"Ye preachers, take him for your joyful theme;
"Take him my dear Americans, he said,
"Be your complaints on his kind bosom laid:
"Take him, ye Africans, he longs for you,
"Impartial Saviour is his title due:
"Wash'd in the fountain of redeeming blood,
"You shall be sons, and kings, and priests to God."
   Great Countess,[3] we Americans revere
Thy name, and mingle in thy grief sincere;
New England deeply feels, the Orphans mourn,
Their more than father will no more return.
   But, though arrested by the hand of death,
Whitefield no more exerts his lab'ring breath,
Yet let us view him in th' eternal skies,
Let ev'ry heart to this bright vision rise;
While the tomb safe retains its sacred trust,
Till life divine re-animates his dust.

---

3 The Countess of Huntingdon, to whom Mr. Whitefield
  was Chaplain.

ON THE DEATH OF A YOUNG
LADY OF FIVE YEARS OF AGE

FROM dark abodes to fair etherial light
Th' enraptur'd innocent has wing'd her flight;
On the kind bosom of eternal love
She finds unknown beatitude above.
This known, ye parents, nor her loss deplore,
She feels the iron hand of pain no more;
The dispensations of unerring grace,
Should turn your sorrows into grateful praise;
Let then no tears for her henceforward flow,
No more distress'd in our dark vale below,
   Her morning sun, which rose divinely bright,
Was quickly mantled with the gloom of night;
But hear in heav'n's blest bow'rs your Nancy fair,
And learn to imitate her language there.
"Thou, Lord, whom I behold with glory crown'd,
"By what sweet name, and in what tuneful sound
"Wilt thou be prais'd? Seraphic pow'rs are faint
"Infinite love and majesty to paint.
"To thee let all their graceful voices raise,
"And saints and angels join their songs of praise."
   Perfect in bliss she from her heav'nly home
Looks down, and smiling beckons you to come;
Why then, fond parents, why these fruitless groans?
Restrain your tears, and cease your plaintive moans.
Freed from a world of sin, and snares, and pain,
Why would you wish your daughter back again?
No—bow resign'd. Let hope your grief control,

And check the rising tumult of the soul.
Calm in the prosperous, and adverse day,
Adore the God who gives and takes away;
Eye him in all, his holy name revere,
Upright your actions, and your hearts sincere,
Till having sail'd through life's tempestuous sea,
And from its rocks, and boist'rous billows free,
Yourselves, safe landed on the blissful shore,
Shall join your happy babe to part no more.

ON THE DEATH OF
A YOUNG GENTLEMAN

WHO taught thee conflict with the pow'rs of night,
To vanquish satan in the fields of light?
Who strung thy feeble arms with might unknown,
How great thy conquest, and how bright thy crown!
War with each princedom, throne, and pow'r is o'er,
The scene is ended to return no more.
O could my muse thy seat on high behold,
How deckt with laurel, how enrich'd with gold!
O could she hear what praise thine harp employs,
How sweet thine anthems, how divine thy joys!
What heav'nly grandeur should exalt her strain!
What holy raptures in her numbers reign!
To sooth the troubles of the mind to peace,
To still the tumult of life's tossing seas,
To ease the anguish of the parents heart,
What shall my sympathizing verse impart?
Where is the balm to heal so deep a wound?
Where shall a sov'reign remedy be found?
Look, gracious Spirit, from thine heav'nly bow'r,
And thy full joys into their bosoms pour;
The raging tempest of their grief control,
And spread the dawn of glory through the soul,
To eye the path the saint departed trod,
And trace him to the bosom of his God.

TO A LADY ON THE
DEATH OF HER HUSBAND

GRIM monarch! see, depriv'd of vital breath,
A young physician in the dust of death:
Dost thou go on incessant to destroy,
Our griefs to double, and lay waste our joy?
Enough thou never yet wast known to say,
Though millions die, the vassals of thy sway:
Nor youth, nor science, not the ties of love,
Nor ought on earth thy flinty heart can move.
The friend, the spouse from his dire dart to save,
In vain we ask the sovereign of the grave.
Fair mourner, there see thy lov'd Leonard laid,
And o'er him spread the deep impervious shade.
Clos'd are his eyes, and heavy fetters keep
His senses bound in never-waking sleep,
Till time shall cease, till many a starry world
Shall fall from heav'n, in dire confusion hurl'd
Till nature in her final wreck shall lie,
And her last groan shall rend the azure sky:
Not, not till then his active soul shall claim
His body, a divine immortal frame.
　But see the softly-stealing tears apace
Pursue each other down the mourner's face;
But cease thy tears, bid ev'ry sigh depart,
And cast the load of anguish from thine heart:
From the cold shell of his great soul arise,
And look beyond, thou native of the skies;
There fix thy view, where fleeter than the wind

39

Thy Leonard mounts, and leaves the earth behind.
Thyself prepare to pass the vale of night
To join for ever on the hills of light:
To thine embrace this joyful spirit moves
To thee, the partner of his earthly loves;
He welcomes thee to pleasures more refin'd,
And better suited to th' immortal mind.

GOLIATH OF GATH

1 SAMUEL, CHAP XVII

YE martial pow'rs, and all ye tuneful nine,
Inspire my song, and aid my high design.
The dreadful scenes and toils of war I write,
The ardent warriors, and the fields of fight:
You best remember, and you best can sing
The acts of heroes to the vocal string:
Resume the lays with which your sacred lyre,
Did then the poet and the sage inspire.
  Now front to front the armies were display'd,
Here Israel rang'd, and there the foes array'd;
The hosts on two opposing mountains stood,
Thick as the foliage of the waving wood;
Between them an extensive valley lay,
O'er which the gleaming armour pour'd the day,
When from the camp of the Philistine foes,
Dreadful to view, a mighty warrior rose;
In the dire deeds of bleeding battle skill'd,
The monster stalks the terror of the field.
From Gath he sprung, Goliath was his name,
Of fierce deportment, and gigantic frame:
A brazen helmet on his head was plac'd,
A coat of mail his form terrific grac'd,
The greaves his legs, the targe his shoulders prest:
Dreadful in arms high-tow'ring o'er the rest
A spear he proudly wav'd, whose iron head,
Strange to relate, six hundred shekels weigh'd;

He strode along, and shook the ample field,
While Phoebus blaz'd refulgent on his shield:
Through Jacob's race a chilling horror ran,
When thus the huge, enormous chief began:
   "Say, what the cause that in this proud array
"You set your battle in the face of day?
"One hero find in all your vaunting train,
"Then see who loses, and who wins the plain;
"For he who wins, in triumph may demand
"Perpetual service from the vanquish'd land:
"Your armies I defy, your force despise,
"By far inferior in Philistia's eyes:
"Produce a man, and let us try the fight,
"Decide the contest, and the victor's right."
   Thus challeng'd he: all Israel stood amaz'd,
And ev'ry chief in consternation gaz'd;
But Jesse's son in youthful bloom appears,
And warlike courage far beyond his years:
He left the folds, he left the flow'ry meads,
And soft recesses of the sylvan shades.
Now Israel's monarch, and his troops arise,
With peals of shouts ascending to the skies;
In Elah's vale the scene of combat lies.
   When the fair morning blush'd with orient red,
What David's fire enjoin'd the son obey'd,
And swift of foot towards the trench he came,
Where glow'd each bosom with the martial flame.
He leaves his carriage to another's care,
And runs to greet his brethren of the war.
While yet they spake the giant-chief arose,
Repeats the challenge, and insults his foes:
Struck with the sound, and trembling at the view,
Affrighted Israel from its post withdrew.
"Observe ye this tremendous foe, they cry'd,
"Who in proud vaunts our armies hath defy'd:

"Whoever lays him prostrate on the plain,
"Freedom in Israel for his house shall gain;
"And on him wealth unknown the king will pour,
"And give his royal daughter for his dow'r."
    Then Jesse's youngest hope: "My brethren say,
"What shall be done for him who takes away
"Reproach from Jacob, who destroys the chief.
"And puts a period to his country's grief.
"He vaunts the honours of his arms abroad,
"And scorns the armies of the living God."
    Thus spoke the youth, th' attentive people ey'd
The wond'rous hero, and again reply'd:
"Such the rewards our monarch will bestow,
"On him who conquers, and destroys his foe."
    Eliab heard, and kindled into ire
To hear his shepherd brother thus inquire,
And thus begun: "What errand brought thee? say
"Who keeps thy flock? or does it go astray?
"I know the base ambition of thine heart,
"But back in safety from the field depart."
    Eliab thus to Jesse's youngest heir,
Express'd his wrath in accents most severe.
When to his brother mildly he reply'd.
"What have I done? or what the cause to chide?
    The words were told before the king, who sent
For the young hero to his royal tent:
Before the monarch dauntless he began,
"For this Philistine fail no heart of man:
"I'll take the vale, and with the giant fight:
"I dread not all his boasts, nor all his might."
    When thus the king: "Dar'st thou a stripling go,
"And venture combat with so great a foe?
"Who all his days has been inur'd to fight,
"And made its deeds his study and delight:
"Battles and bloodshed brought the monster forth,

"And clouds and whirlwinds usher'd in his birth."
    When David thus: "I kept the fleecy care,
"And out there rush'd a lion and a bear;
"A tender lamb the hungry lion took,
"And with no other weapon than my crook
"Bold I pursu'd, and chas d him o'er the field,
"The prey deliver'd, and the felon kill'd:
"As thus the lion and the bear I slew,
"So shall Goliath fall, and all his crew:
"The God, who sav'd me from these beasts of prey,
"By me this monster in the dust shall lay."
    So David spoke. The wond'ring king reply'd;
"Go thou with heav'n and victory on thy side:
"This coat of mail, this sword gird on," he said,
And plac'd a mighty helmet on his head:
The coat, the sword, the helm he laid aside,
Nor chose to venture with those arms untry'd,
Then took his staff, and to the neighb'ring brook
Instant he ran, and thence five pebbles took.
Mean time descended to Philistia's son
A radiant cherub, and he thus begun:
"Goliath, well thou know'st thou hast defy'd
"Yon Hebrew armies, and their God deny'd:
"Rebellious wretch! audacious worm! forbear,
"Nor tempt the vengeance of their God too far:
"Them, who with his Omnipotence contend,
"No eye shall pity, and no arm defend:
"Proud as thou art, in short liv'd glory great,
"I come to tell thee thine approaching fate.
"Regard my words. The Judge of all the gods,
"Beneath whose steps the tow'ring mountain nods,
"Will give thine armies to the savage brood,
"That cut the liquid air, or range the wood.
"Thee too a well-aim'd pebble shall destroy,
"And thou shalt perish by a beardless boy:

"Such is the mandate from the realms above,
"And should I try the vengeance to remove,
"Myself a rebel to my king would prove.
"Goliath say, shall grace to him be shown,
"Who dares heav'ns Monarch, and insults his throne?"
　"Your words are lost on me," the giant cries,
While fear and wrath contended in his eyes,
When thus the messenger from heav'n replies:
"Provoke no more Jehovah's awful hand
"To hurl its vengeance on thy guilty land:
"He grasps the thunder, and, he wings the storm,
"Servants their sov'reign's orders to perform."
　The angel spoke, and turn'd his eyes away,
Adding new radiance to the rising day.
　Now David comes: the fatal stones demand
His left, the staff engag'd his better hand:
The giant mov'd, and from his tow'ring height
Survey'd the stripling, and disdain'd the fight,
And thus began: "Am I a dog with thee?
"Bring'st thou no armour, but a staff to me?
"The gods on thee their vollied curses pour,
"And beasts and birds of prey thy flesh devour."
　David undaunted thus, "Thy spear and shield
"Shall no protection to thy body yield:
"Jehovah's name—no other arms I bear,
"I ask no other in this glorious war.
"To-day the Lord of Hosts to me will give
"Vict'ry, to-day thy doom thou shalt receive;
"The fate you threaten shall your own become,
"And beasts shall be your animated tomb,
"That all the earth's inhabitants may know
"That there's a God, who governs all below:
"This great assembly too shall witness stand,
"That needs nor sword, nor spear, th' Almighty's hand:
"The battle his, the conquest he bestows,

"And to our pow'r consigns our hated foes."
  Thus David spoke; Goliath heard and came
To meet the hero in the field of fame.
Ah! fatal meeting to thy troops and thee,
But thou wast deaf to the divine decree;
Young David meets thee, meets thee not in vain;
'Tis thine to perish on th' ensanguin'd plain.
  And now the youth the forceful pebble slung
Philistia trembled as it whizz'd along:
In his dread forehead, where the helmet ends,
Just o'er the brows the well-aim'd stone descends,
It pierc'd the skull, and shatter'd all the brain,
Prone on his face he tumbled to the plain:
Goliath's fall no smaller terror yields
Than riving thunders in aerial fields:
The soul still ling'red in its lov'd abode,
Till conq'ring David o'er the giant strode:
Goliath's sword then laid its master dead,
And from the body hew'd the ghastly head;
The blood in gushing torrents drench'd the plains,
The soul found passage through the spouting veins.
  And now aloud th' illustrious victor said,
"Where are your boastings now your champion's "dead?"
  Scarce had he spoke, when the Philistines fled:
But fled in vain; the conqu'ror swift pursu'd:
What scenes of slaughter! and what seas of blood!
There Saul thy thousands grasp'd th' impurpled sand
In pangs of death the conquest of thine hand;
And David there were thy ten thousands laid:
Thus Israel's damsels musically play'd.
  Near Gath and Edron many an hero lay,
Breath'd out their souls, and curs'd the light of day:
Their fury, quench'd by death, no longer burns,
And David with Goliath's head returns,
To Salem brought, but in his tent he plac'd

The load of armour which the giant grac'd.
His monarch saw him coming from the war,
And thus demanded of the son of Ner.
"Say, who is this amazing youth?" he cry'd,
When thus the leader of the host reply'd;
"As lives thy soul I know not whence he sprung,
"So great in prowess though in years so young:"
   "Inquire whose son is he," the sov'reign said,
"Before whose conq'ring arm Philistia fled."
   Before the king behold the stripling stand,
Goliath's head depending from his hand:
To him the king: "Say of what martial line
"Art thou, young hero, and what sire was thine?"
He humbly thus; "The son of Jesse I:
"I came the glories of the field to try.
"Small is my tribe, but valiant in the fight;
"Small is my city, but thy royal right."
   "Then take the promis'd gifts," the monarch cry'd,
Conferring riches and the royal bride:
"Knit to my soul for ever thou remain
"With me, nor quit my regal roof again."

THOUGHTS ON THE
WORKS OF PROVIDENCE

ARISE, my soul, on wings enraptur'd, rise
To praise the monarch of the earth and skies,
Whose goodness and benificence appear
As round its centre moves the rolling year,
Or when the morning glows with rosy charms,
Or the sun slumbers in the ocean's arms:
Of light divine be a rich portion lent
To guide my soul, and favour my intend.
Celestial muse, my arduous flight sustain
And raise my mind to a seraphic strain!
    Ador'd for ever be the God unseen,
Which round the sun revolves this vast machine,
Though to his eye its mass a point appears:
Ador'd the God that whirls surrounding spheres,
Which first ordain'd that mighty Sol should reign
The peerless monarch of th' ethereal train:
Of miles twice forty millions is his height,
And yet his radiance dazzles mortal sight
So far beneath—from him th' extended earth
Vigour derives, and ev'ry flow'ry birth:
Vast through her orb she moves with easy grace
Around her Phoebus in unbounded space;
True to her course th' impetuous storm derides,
Triumphant o'er the winds, and surging tides.
    Almighty, in these wond'rous works of thine,
What Pow'r, what Wisdom, and what Goodness shine!
And are thy wonders, Lord, by men explor'd,

And yet creating glory unador'd!
  Creation smiles in various beauty gay,
While day to night, and night succeeds to day:
That Wisdom, which attends Jehovah's ways,
Shines most conspicuous in the solar rays:
Without them, destitute of heat and light,
This world would be the reign of endless night:
In their excess how would our race complain,
Abhorring life! how hate its length'ned chain!
From air adust what num'rous ills would rise?
What dire contagion taint the burning skies?
What pestilential vapours, fraught with death,
Would rise, and overspread the lands beneath?
  Hail, smiling morn, that from the orient main
Ascending dost adorn the heav'nly plain!
So rich, so various are thy beauteous dies,
That spread through all the circuit of the skies,
That, full of thee, my soul in rapture soars,
And thy great God, the cause of all adores.
  O'er beings infinite his love extends,
His Wisdom rules them, and his Pow'r defends.
When tasks diurnal tire the human frame,
The spirits faint, and dim the vital flame,
Then too that ever active bounty shines,
Which not infinity of space confines.
The sable veil, that Night in silence draws,
Conceals effects, but shows th' Almighty Cause,
Night seals in sleep the wide creation fair,
And all is peaceful but the brow of care.
Again, gay Phoebus, as the day before,
Wakes ev'ry eye, but what shall wake no more;
Again the face of nature is renew'd,
Which still appears harmonious, fair, and good.
May grateful strains salute the smiling morn,
Before its beams the eastern hills adorn!

Shall day to day, and night to night conspire
To show the goodness of the Almighty Sire?
This mental voice shall man regardless hear,
And never, never raise the filial pray'r?
To-day, O hearken, nor your folly mourn
For time mispent, that never will return.
    But see the sons of vegetation rise,
And spread their leafy banners to the skies.
All-wise Almighty Providence we trace
In trees, and plants, and all the flow'ry race;
As clear as in the nobler frame of man,
All lovely copies of the Maker's plan.
The pow'r the same that forms a ray of light,
That call d creation from eternal night.
"Let there be light," he said: from his profound
Old Chaos heard, and trembled at the sound:
Swift as the word, inspir'd by pow'r divine,
Behold the light around its Maker shine,
The first fair product of th' omnific God,
And now through all his works diffus'd abroad.
    As reason's pow'rs by day our God disclose,
So we may trace him in the night's repose:
Say what is sleep? and dreams how passing strange!
When action ceases, and ideas range
Licentious and unbounded o'er the plains,
Where Fancy's queen in giddy triumph reigns.
Hear in soft strains the dreaming lover sigh
To a kind fair, or rave in jealousy;
On pleasure now, and now on vengeance bent,
The lab'ring passions struggle for a vent.
What pow'r, O man! thy reason then restores,
So long suspended in nocturnal hours?
What secret hand returns the mental train,
And gives improv'd thine active pow'rs again?
From thee, O man, what gratitude should rise!

And, when from balmy sleep thou op'st thine eyes,
Let thy first thoughts be praises to the skies.
How merciful our God who thus imparts
O'erflowing tides of joy to human hearts,
When wants and woes might be our righteous lot,
Our God forgetting, by our God forgot!
   Among the mental pow'rs a question rose,
"What most the image of th' Eternal shows?"
When thus to Reason (so let Fancy rove)
Her great companion spoke immortal Love.

   "Say, mighty pow'r, how long shall strife prevail,
"And with its murmurs load the whisp'ring gale?
"Refer the cause to Recollection's shrine,
"Who loud proclaims my origin divine,
"The cause whence heav'n and earth began to be,
"And is not man immortaliz'd by me?
"Reason let this most causeless strife subside."
Thus Love pronounc'd, and Reason thus reply'd.

   "Thy birth, coelestial queen! 'tis mine to own,
"In thee resplendent is the Godhead shown;
"Thy words persuade, my soul enraptur'd feels
"Resistless beauty which thy smile reveals."
Ardent she spoke, and, kindling at her charms,
She clasp'd the blooming goddess in her arms.

   Infinite Love where'er we turn our eyes
Appears: this ev'ry creature's wants supplies;
This most is heard in Nature's constant voice,
This makes the morn, and this the eve rejoice;
This bids the fost'ring rains and dews descend
To nourish all, to serve one gen'ral end,
The good of man: yet man ungrateful pays
But little homage, and but little praise.
To him, whose works arry'd with mercy shine,
What songs should rise, how constant, how divine!

TO A LADY ON THE
DEATH OF THREE RELATIONS

WE trace the pow'r of Death from tomb to tomb,
And his are all the ages yet to come.
'Tis his to call the planets from on high,
To blacken Phoebus, and dissolve the sky;
His too, when all in his dark realms are hurl'd,
From its firm base to shake the solid world;
His fatal sceptre rules the spacious whole,
And trembling nature rocks from pole to pole.
    Awful he moves, and wide his wings are spread:
Behold thy brother number'd with the dead!
From bondage freed, the exulting spirit flies
Beyond Olympus, and these starry skies.
Lost in our woe for thee, blest shade, we mourn
In vain; to earth thou never must return.
Thy sisters too, fair mourner, feel the dart
Of Death, and with fresh torture rend thine heart.
Weep not for them, and leave the world behind.
    As a young plant by hurricanes up torn,
So near its parent lies the newly born—
But 'midst the bright ehtereal train behold
It shines superior on a throne of gold:
Then, mourner, cease; let hope thy tears restrain,
Smile on the tomb, and sooth the raging pain.
On yon blest regions fix thy longing view,
Mindless of sublunary scenes below;
Ascend the sacred mount, in thought arise,
And seek substantial and immortal joys;

Where hope receives, where faith to vision springs,
And raptur'd seraphs tune th' immortal strings
To strains extatic. Thou the chorus join,
And to thy father tune the praise divine.

TO A CLERGYMAN ON
THE DEATH OF HIS LADY

WHERE contemplation finds her sacred spring,
Where heav'nly music makes the arches ring,
Where virtue reigns unsully'd and divine,
Where wisdom thron'd, and all the graces shine,
There sits thy spouse amidst the radiant throng,
While praise eternal warbles from her tongue;
There choirs angelic shout her welcome round,
With perfect bliss, and peerless glory crown'd.
    While thy dear mate, to flesh no more confin'd,
Exults a blest, an heav'n-ascended mind,
Say in thy breast shall floods of sorrow rise?
Say shall its torrents overwhelm thine eyes?
Amid the seats of heav'n a place is free,
And angels open their bright ranks for thee;
For thee they wait, and with expectant eye
Thy spouse leans downward from th' empyreal sky:
"O come away," her longing spirit cries,
"And share with me the raptures of the skies.
"Our bliss divine to mortals is unknown;
"Immortal life and glory are our own.
"There too may the dear pledges of our love
"Arrive, and taste with us the joys above;
"Attune the harp to more than mortal lays,
"And join with us the tribute of their praise
"To him, who dy'd stern justice to stone,
"And make eternal glory all our own.
"He in his death slew ours, and, as he rose,

54

"He crush'd the dire dominion of our foes;
"Vain were their hopes to put the God to flight,
"Chain us to hell, and bar the gates of light."
   She spoke, and turn'd from mortal scenes her eyes,
Which beam'd celestial radiance o'er the skies.
   Then thou dear man, no more with grief retire,
Let grief no longer damp devotion's fire,
But rise sublime, to equal bliss aspire,
Thy sighs no more be wafted by the wind,
No more complain, but be to heav'n resign'd
'Twas thine t' unfold the oracles divine,
To sooth our woes the task was also thine;
Now sorrow is incumbent on thy heart,
Permit the muse a cordial to impart;
Who can to thee their tend'rest aid refuse?
To dry thy tears how longs the heav'nly muse

AN HYMN TO
THE MORNING

ATTEND my lays, ye ever honour'd nine,
Assist my labours, and my strains refine;
In smoothest numbers pour the notes along,
For bright Aurora now demands my song.
  Aurora hail, and all the thousand dies,
Which deck thy progress through the vaulted skies:
The morn awakes, and wide extends her rays,
On ev'ry leaf the gentle zephyr plays;
Harmonious lays the feather'd race resume,
Dart the bright eye, and shake the painted plume.
  Ye shady groves, your verdant gloom display
To shield your poet from the burning day:
Calliope awake the sacred lyre,
While thy fair sisters fan the pleasing fire:
The bow'rs, the gales, the variegated skies
In all their pleasures in my bosom rise.
  See in the east th' illustrious king of day!
His rising radiance drives the shades away—
But Oh! I feel his fervid beams too strong,
And scarce begun, concludes th' abortive song.

AN HYMN TO
THE EVENING

SOON as the sun forsook the eastern main
The pealing thunder shook the heav'nly plain;
Majestic grandeur! From the zephyr's wing,
Exhales the incense of the blooming spring.
Soft purl the streams, the birds renew their notes,
And through the air their mingled music floats.
  Through all the heav'ns what beauteous dies are spread!
But the west glories in the deepest red:
So may our breasts with ev'ry virtue glow,
The living temples of our God below!
  Fill'd with the praise of him who gives the light,
And draws the sable curtains of the night,
Let placid slumbers sooth each weary mind,
At morn to wake more heav'nly, more refin'd;
So shall the labours of the day begin
More pure, more guarded from the snares of sin.
  Night's leaden sceptre seals my drowsy eyes,
Then cease, my song, till fair Aurora rise.

ISAIAH
LXIII 1 - 8

SAY, heav'nly muse, what king or mighty God,
That moves sublime from Idumea's road?
In Bosrah's dies, with martial glories join'd,
His purple vesture waves upon the wind.
Why thus enrob'd delights he to appear
In the dread image of the Pow'r of war?
　　Compres'd in wrath the swelling wine-press groan'd,
It bled, and pour'd the gushing purple round.
　　"Mine was the act," th' Almighty Saviour said,
And shook the dazzling glories of his head,
"When all forsook I trod the press alone,
"And conquer'd by omnipotence my own;
"For man's release sustain'd the pond'rous load,
"For man the wrath of an immortal God:
"To execute th' Eternal's dread command
"My soul I sacrific'd with willing hand;
"Sinless I stood before the avenging frown,
"Atoning thus for vices not my own."
　　His eye the ample field of battle round
Survey'd, but no created succours found;
His own omnipotence sustain'd the right,
His vengeance sunk the haughty foes in night;
Beneath his feet the prostrate troops were spread,
And round him lay the dying, and the dead.
　　Great God, what light'ning flashes from thine eyes?
What pow'r withstands if thou indignant rise?
　　Against thy Zion though her foes may rage,

And all their cunning, all their strength engage,
Yet she serenely on thy bosom lies,
Smiles at their arts, and all their force defies.

ON RECOLLECTION

MNEME begin. Inspire, ye sacred nine,
Your vent'rous Afric in her great design.
Mneme, immortal pow'r, I trace thy spring:
Assist my strains, while I thy glories sing:
The acts of long departed years, by thee
Recover'd, in due order rang'd we see:
Thy pow'r the long-forgotten calls from night,
That sweetly plays before the fancy's sight.
Mneme in our nocturnal visions pours
The ample treasure of her secret stores;
Swift from above the wings her silent flight
Through Phoebe's realms, fair regent of the night;
And, in her pomp of images display'd,
To the high-raptur'd poet gives her aid,
Through the unbounded regions of the mind,
Diffusing light celestial and refin'd.
The heav'nly phantom paints the actions done
By ev'ry tribe beneath the rolling sun.
   Mneme, enthron'd within the human breast,
Has vice condemn'd, and ev'ry virtue blest.
How sweet the sound when we her plaudit hear?
Sweeter than music to the ravish'd ear,
Sweeter than Maro's entertaining strains
Resounding through the groves, and hills, and plains.
But how is Mneme dreaded by the race,
Who scorn her warnings and despise her grace?
By her unveil'd each horrid crime appears,
Her awful hand a cup of wormwood bears.
Days, years mispent, O what a hell of woe!

Hers the worst tortures that our souls can know.
　Now eighteen years their destin'd course have run,
In fast succession round the central sun.
How did the follies of that period pass
Unnotic'd, but behold them writ in brass!
In Recollection see them fresh return,
And sure 'tis mine to be asham'd, and mourn.
　O Virtue, smiling in immortal green,
Do thou exert thy pow'r, and change the scene;
Be thine employ to guide my future days,
And mine to pay the tribute of my praise.
　Of Recollection such the pow'r enthron'd
In ev'ry breast, and thus her pow'r is own'd.
The wretch, who dar'd the vengeance of the skies,
At last awakes in horror and surprise,
By her alarm'd, he sees impending fate,
He howls in anguish, and repents too late.
But O! what peace, what joys are hers t' impart
To ev'ry holy, ev'ry upright heart!
Thrice blest the man, who, in her sacred shrine,
Feels himself shelter'd from the wrath divine!

ON IMAGINATION

THY various works, imperial queen, we see,
   How bright their forms! how deck'd with pomp by thee!
Thy wond'rous acts in beauteous order stand,
And all attest how potent is thine hand.
   From Helicon's refulgent heights attend,
Ye sacred choir, and my attempts befriend:
To tell her glories with a faithful tongue,
Ye blooming graces, triumph in my song.
   Now here, now there, the roving Fancy flies,
Till some lov'd object strikes her wand'ring eyes,
Whose silken fetters all the senses bind,
And soft captivity involves the mind.
   Imagination! who can sing thy force?
Or who describe the swiftness of thy course?
Soaring through air to find the bright abode,
Th' empyreal palace of the thund'ring God,
We on thy pinions can surpass the wind,
And leave the rolling universe behind:
From star to star the mental optics rove,
Measure the skies, and range the realms above.
There in one view we grasp the mighty whole,
Or with new worlds amaze th' unbounded soul.
   Though Winter frowns to Fancy's raptur'd eyes
The fields may flourish, and gay scenes arise;
The frozen deeps may break their iron bands,
And bid their waters murmur o'er the sands.
Fair Flora may resume her fragrant reign,
And with her flow'ry riches deck the plain;
Sylvanus may diffuse his honours round,

And all the forest may with leaves be crown'd:
Show'rs may descend, and dews their gems disclose,
And nectar sparkle on the blooming rose.
　　Such is thy pow'r, nor are thine orders vain,
O thou the leader of the mental train:
In full perfection all thy works are wrought,
And thine the sceptre o'er the realms of thought.
Before thy throne the subject-passions bow,
Of subject-passions sov'reign ruler thou;
At thy command joy rushes on the heart,
And through the glowing veins the spirits dart.
　　Fancy might now her silken pinions try
To rise from earth, and sweep th' expanse on high:
From Tithon's bed now might Aurora rise,
Her cheeks all glowing with celestial dies,
While a pure stream of light o'erflows the skies.
The monarch of the day I might behold,
And all the mountains tipt with radiant gold,
But I reluctant leave the pleasing views,
Which Fancy dresses to delight the Muse;
Winter austere forbids me to aspire,
And northern tempests damp the rising fire;
They chill the tides of Fancy's flowing sea,
Cease then, my song, cease the unequal lay.

A FUNERAL POEM
ON THE DEATH OF C. E.

AN INFANT OF TWELVE MONTHS

THROUGH airy roads he wings his instant flight
To purer regions of celestial light;
Enlarg'd he sees unnumber'd systems roll,
Beneath him sees the universal whole,
Planets on planets run their destin'd round,
And circling wonders fill the vast profound.
Th' ethereal now, and now th' empyreal skies
With growing splendors strike his wond'ring eyes:
The angels view him with delight unknown,
Press his soft hand, and seat him on his throne;
Then smilling thus: "To this divine abode,
"The seat of saints, of seraphs, and of God,
"Thrice welcome thou." The raptur'd babe replies,
"Thanks to my God, who snatch'd me to the skies,
"E'er vice triumphant had possess'd my heart,
"E'er yet the tempter had beguil d my heart,
"E'er yet on sin's base actions I was bent,
"E'er yet I knew temptation's dire intent;
"E'er yet the lash for horrid crimes I felt,
"E'er vanity had led my way to guilt,
"But, soon arriv'd at my celestial goal,
"Full glories rush on my expanding soul."
Joyful he spoke: exulting cherubs round
Clapt their glad wings, the heav'nly vaults resound.
    Say, parents, why this unavailing moan?

64

Why heave your pensive bosoms with the groan?
To Charles, the happy subject of my song,
A brighter world, and nobler strains belong.
Say would you tear him from the realms above
By thoughtless wishes, and prepost'rous love?
Doth his felicity increase your pain?
Or could you welcome to this world again
The heir of bliss? with a superior air
Methinks he answers with a smile severe,
"Thrones and dominions cannot tempt me there."
  But still you cry, "Can we the sigh forbear,
"And still and still must we not pour the tear?
"Our only hope, more dear than vital breath,
"Twelve moons revolv'd, becomes the prey of death;
"Delightful infant, nightly visions give
"Thee to our arms, and we with joy receive,
"We fain would clasp the Phantom to our breast,
"The Phantom flies, and leaves the soul unblest."
  To yon bright regions let your faith ascend,
Prepare to join your dearest infant friend
In pleasures without measure, without end.

TO CAPTAIN H—D

OF THE 65TH REGIMENT

SAY, muse divine, can hostile scenes delight
The warrior's bosom in the fields of fight?
Lo! here the christian and the hero join
With mutual grace to form the man divine.
In H—D see with pleasure and surprise,
Where valour kindles, and where virtue lies:
Go, hero brave, still grace the post of fame,
And add new glories to thine honour'd name,
Still to the field, and still to virtue true:
Britannia glories in no son like you.

TO THE RIGHT
HONOURABLE WILLIAM

EARL OF DARTMOUTH

**His Majesty's Principal
Secretary of State for North-America, &c.**

HAIL, happy day, when, smiling like the morn,
Fair Freedom rose New-England to adorn:
The northern clime beneath her genial ray,
Dartmouth, congratulates thy blissful sway:
Elate with hope her race no longer mourns,
Each soul expands, each grateful bosom burns,
While in thine hand with pleasure we behold
The silken reins, and Freedom's charms unfold.
Long lost to realms beneath the northern skies
She shines supreme, while hated faction dies:
Soon as appear'd the Goddess long desir'd,
Sick at the view, she languish'd and expir'd;
Thus from the splendors of the morning light
The owl in sadness seeks the caves of night.
    No more, America, in mournful strain
Of wrongs, and grievance unredress'd complain,
No longer shalt thou dread the iron chain,
Which wanton Tyranny with lawless hand
Had made, and with it meant t' enslave the land.
    Should you, my lord, while you peruse my song,
Wonder from whence my love of Freedom sprung,
Whence flow these wishes for the common good,

By feeling hearts alone best understood,
I, young in life, by seeming cruel fate
Was snatch'd from Afric's fancy'd happy seat:
What pangs excruciating must molest,
What sorrows labour in my parent's breast?
Steel'd was that soul and by no misery mov'd
That from a father seiz'd his babe belov'd:
Such, such my case. And can I then but pray
Others may never feel tyrannic sway?
   For favours past, great Sir, our thanks are due,
And thee we ask thy favours to renew,
Since in thy pow'r, as in thy will before,
To sooth the griefs, which thou did'st once deplore.
May heav'nly grace the sacred sanction give
To all thy works, and thou for ever live
Not only on the wings of fleeting Fame,
Though praise immortal crowns the patriot's name,
But to conduct to heav'ns refulgent fane,
May fiery coursers sweep th' ethereal plain,
And bear thee upwards to that blest abode,
Where, like the prophet, thou shalt find thy God.

ODE TO NEPTUNE

ON MRS. W—'S VOYAGE TO ENGLAND

I

WHILE raging tempests shake the shore,
While AElus' thunders round us roar,
And sweep impetuous o'er the plain
Be still, O tyrant of the main;
Nor let thy brow contracted frowns betray,
While my Susanna skims the wat'ry way.

II

The Pow'r propitious hears the lay,
The blue-ey'd daughters of the sea
With sweeter cadence glide along,
And Thames responsive joins the song.
Pleas'd with their notes Sol sheds benign his ray,
And double radiance decks the face of day.

III

To court thee to Britannia's arms
   Serene the climes and mild the sky,
Her region boasts unnumber'd charms,
   Thy welcome smiles in ev'ry eye.
Thy promise, Neptune keep, record my pray'r,
Not give my wishes to the empty air.

Boston, October 12, 1772.

TO A LADY ON HER COMING TO NORTH-AMERICA WITH HER SON

FOR THE RECOVERY OF HER HEALTH

INDULGENT muse! my grov'ling mind inspire,
And fill my bosom with celestial fire.
See from Jamaica's fervid shore she moves,
Like the fair mother of the blooming loves,
When from above the Goddess with her hand
Fans the soft breeze, and lights upon the land;
Thus she on Neptune's wat'ry realm reclin'd
Appear'd, and thus invites the ling'ring wind.
    "Arise, ye winds, America explore,
"Waft me, ye gales, from this malignant shore;
"The Northern milder climes I long to greet,
"There hope that health will my arrival meet."
Soon as she spoke in my ideal view
The winds assented, and the vessel flew.
    Madam, your spouse bereft of wife and son,
In the grove's dark recesses pours his moan;
Each branch, wide-spreading to the ambient sky,
Forgets its verdure, and submits to die.
    From thence I turn, and leave the sultry plain,
And swift pursue thy passage o'er the main:
The ship arrives before the fav'ring wind,
And makes the Philadelphian port assign'd,
Thence I attend you to Bostonia's arms,
Where gen'rous friendship ev'ry bosom warms:

71

Thrice welcome here! may health revive again,
Bloom on thy cheek, and bound in ev'ry vein!
Then back return to gladden ev'ry heart,
And give your spouse his soul's far dearer part,
Receiv'd again with what a sweet surprise,
The tear in transport starting from his eyes!
While his attendant son with blooming grace
Springs to his father's ever dear embrace.
With shouts of joy Jamaica's rocks resound,
With shouts of joy the country rings around.

TO A LADY ON HER
REMARKABLE PRESERVATION IN
AN HURRICANE IN NORTH-CAROLINA

THOUGH thou did'st hear the tempest from afar,
And felt'st the horrors of the wat'ry war,
To me unknown, yet on this peaceful shore
Methinks I hear the storm tumultuous roar,
And how stern Boreas with impetuous hand
Compell'd the Nereids to usurp the land.
Reluctant rose the daughters of the main,
And slow ascending glided o'er the plain,
Till AEolus in his rapid chariot drove
In gloomy grandeur from the vault above:
Furious he comes. His winged sons obey
Their frantic sire, and madden all the sea.
The billows rave, the wind's fierce tyrant roars,
And with his thund'ring terrors shakes the shores:
Broken by waves the vessel's frame is rent,
And strows with planks the wat'ry element.
   But thee, Maria, a kind Nereid's shield
Preserv'd from sinking, and thy form upheld:
And sure some heav'nly oracle design'd
At that dread crisis to instruct thy mind
Things of eternal consequence to weigh,
And to thine heart just feelings to convey
Of things above, and of the future doom,
And what the births of the dread world to come.
   From tossing seas I welcome thee to land.
"Resign her, Nereid," 'twas thy God's command.

Thy spouse late buried, as thy fears conceiv'd,
Again returns, thy fears are all reliev'd:
Thy daughter blooming with superior grace
Again thou see'st, again thine arms embrace;
O come, and joyful show thy spouse his heir,
And what the blessings of maternal care!

TO A LADY
AND HER CHILDREN

ON THE DEATH OF HER
SON AND THEIR BROTHER

O'ERWHELMING sorrow now demands my song:
From death the overwhelming sorrow sprung.
What flowing tears? What hearts with grief opprest?
What sighs on sighs heave the fond parent's breast?
The brother weeps, the hapless sisters join
Th' increasing woe, and swell the crystal brine;
The poor, who once his gen'rous bounty fed,
Droop, and bewail their benefactor dead.
In death the friend, the kind companion lies,
And in one death what various comfort dies!
  Th' unhappy mother sees the sanguine rill
Forget to flow, and nature's wheels stand still,
But see from earth his spirit far remov'd,
And know no grief recals your best-belov'd:
He, upon pinions swifter than the wind,
Has left mortality's sad scenes behind
For joys to this terrestial state unknown,
And glories richer than the monarch's crown.
Of virtue's steady course the prize behold!
What blissful wonders to his mind unfold!
But of celestial joys I sing in vain:
Attempt not, muse, the too advent'rous strain.
  No more in briny show'rs, ye friends around,
Or bathe his clay, or waste them on the ground:

75

Still do you weep, still wish for his return?
How cruel thus to wish, and thus to mourn?
No more for him the streams of sorrow pour,
But haste to join him on the heav'nly shore,
On harps of gold to tune immortal lays,
And to your God immortal anthems raise.

TO A GENTLEMAN
AND LADY ON THE DEATH
OF THE LADY'S BROTHER AND SISTER

AND A CHILD OF
THE NAME OF AVIS, AGED ONE YEAR

ON Death's domain intent I fix my eyes,
Where human nature in vast ruin lies:
With pensive mind I search the drear abode,
Where the great conqu'ror has his spoils bestow'd;
There where the offspring of six thousand years
In endless numbers to my view appears:
Whole kingdoms in his gloomy den are thrust,
And nations mix with their primeval dust:
Insatiate still he gluts the ample tomb;
His is the present, his the age to come.
See here a brother, here a sister spread,
And a sweet daughter mingled with the dead.
   But, Madam, let your grief be laid aside,
And let the fountain of your tears be dry'd,
In vain they flow to wet the dusty plain,
Your sighs are wafted to the skies in vain,
Your pains they witness, but they can no more,
While Death reigns tyrant o'er this mortal shore.
   The glowing stars and silver queen of light
At last must perish in the gloom of night:
Resign thy friends to that Almighty hand,
Which gave them life, and bow to his command;
Thine Avis give without a murm'ring heart,

Though half thy soul be fated to depart.
To shining guards consign thine infant care
To waft triumphant through the seas of air:
Her soul enlarg'd to heav'nly pleasure springs,
She feeds on truth and uncreated things.
Methinks I hear her in the realms above,
And leaning forward with a filial love,
Invite you there to share immortal bliss
Unknown, untasted in a state like this.
With tow'ring hopes, and growing grace arise,
And seek beatitude beyond the skies.

ON THE DEATH OF
DR. SAMUEL MARSHALL

1771

THROUGH thickest glooms look back, immortal shade,
On that confusion which thy death has made:
Or from Olympus' height look down, and see
A Town involv'd in grief bereft of thee.
Thy Lucy sees thee mingle with the dead,
And rends the graceful tresses from her head,
Wild in her woe, with grief unknown opprest
Sigh follows sigh deep heaving from her breast.
  Too quickly fled, ah! whither art thou gone?
Ah! lost for ever to thy wife and son!
The hapless child, thine only hope and heir,
Clings round his mother's neck, and weeps his sorrows there.
The loss of thee on Tyler's soul returns,
And Boston for her dear physician mourns.
  When sickness call'd for Marshall's healing hand,
With what compassion did his soul expand?
In him we found the father and the friend:
In life how lov'd! how honour'd in his end!
  And must not then our AEsculapius stay
To bring his ling'ring infant into day?
The babe unborn in the dark womb is tost,
And seems in anguish for its father lost.
  Gone is Apollo from his house of earth,
But leaves the sweet memorials of his worth:
The common parent, whom we all deplore,

From yonder world unseen must come no more,
Yet 'midst our woes immortal hopes attend
The spouse, the sire, the universal friend.

TO A GENTLEMAN ON HIS VOYAGE TO GREAT-BRITAIN

FOR THE RECOVERY OF HIS HEALTH

WHILE others chant of gay Elysian scenes,
Of balmy zephyrs, and of flow'ry plains,
My song more happy speaks a greater name,
Feels higher motives and a nobler flame.
For thee, OR—, the muse attunes her strings,
And mounts sublime above inferior things.
   I sing not now of green embow'ring woods,
I sing not now the daughters of the floods,
I sing not of the storms o'er ocean driv'n,
And how they howl'd along the waste of heav'n.
But I to R— would paint the British shore,
And vast Atlantic, not untry'd before:
Thy life impair'd commands thee to arise,
Leave these bleak regions and inclement skies,
Where chilling winds return the winter past,
And nature shudders at the furious blast.
   O thou stupendous, earth-enclosing main
Exert thy wonders to the world again!
If ere thy pow'r prolong'd the fleeting breath,
Turn'd back the shafts, and mock'd the gates of death,
If ere thine air dispens'd an healing pow'r,
Or snatch'd the victim from the fatal hour,
This equal case demands thine equal care,
And equal wonders may this patient share.
But unavailing, frantic is the dream

To hope thine aid without the aid of him
Who gave thee birth and taught thee where to flow,
And in thy waves his various blessings show.
    May R— return to view his native shore
Replete with vigour not his own before,
Then shall we see with pleasure and surprise,
And own thy work, great Ruler of the skies!

TO THE
REV. DR. THOMAS AMORY

ON READING HIS SERMONS ON
DAILY DEVOTION, IN WHICH THAT DUTY
IS RECOMMENDED AND ASSISTED

TO cultivate in ev'ry noble mind
Habitual grace, and sentiments refin'd,
Thus while you strive to mend the human heart,
Thus while the heav'nly precepts you impart,
O may each bosom catch the sacred fire,
And youthful minds to Virtue's throne aspire!
　　When God's eternal ways you set in sight,
And Virtue shines in all her native light,
In vain would Vice her works in night conceal,
For Wisdom's eye pervades the sable veil.
　　Artists may paint the sun's effulgent rays,
But Amory's pen the brighter God displays:
While his great works in Amory's pages shine,
And while he proves his essence all divine,
The Atheist sure no more can boast aloud
Of chance, or nature, and exclude the God;
As if the clay without the potter's aid
Should rise in various forms, and shapes self-made,
Or worlds above with orb o'er orb profound
Self-mov'd could run the everlasting round.
It cannot be—unerring Wisdom guides
With eye propitious, and o'er all presides.
　　Still prosper, Amory! still may'st thou receive

The warmest blessings which a muse can give,
And when this transitory state is o'er,
When kingdoms fall, and fleeting Fame's no more,
May Amory triumph in immortal fame,
A nobler title, and superior name!

ON THE DEATH OF J. C.

AN INFANT

NO more the flow'ry scenes of pleasure rife,
Nor charming prospects greet the mental eyes,
No more with joy we view that lovely face
Smiling, disportive, flush'd with ev'ry grace.
　The tear of sorrow flows from ev'ry eye,
Groans answer groans, and sighs to sighs reply;
What sudden pangs shot thro' each aching heart,
When, Death, thy messenger dispatch'd his dart?
Thy dread attendants, all-destroying Pow'r,
Hurried the infant to his mortal hour.
Could'st thou unpitying close those radiant eyes?
Or fail'd his artless beauties to surprise?
Could not his innocence thy stroke controul,
Thy purpose shake, and soften all thy soul?
　The blooming babe, with shades of Death o'er-spread,
No more shall smile, no more shall raise its head,
But, like a branch that from the tree is torn,
Falls prostrate, wither'd, languid, and forlorn.
"Where flies my James?" 'tis thus I seem to hear
The parent ask, "Some angel tell me where
"He wings his passage thro' the yielding air?"
Methinks a cherub bending from the skies
Observes the question, and serene replies,
"In heav'ns high palaces your babe appears:
"Prepare to meet him, and dismiss your tears."
Shall not th' intelligence your grief restrain,

85

And turn the mournful to the cheerful strain?
Cease your complaints, suspend each rising sigh,
Cease to accuse the Ruler of the sky.
Parents, no more indulge the falling tear:
Let Faith to heav'n's refulgent domes repair,
There see your infant, like a seraph glow:
What charms celestial in his numbers flow
Melodious, while the foul-enchanting strain
Dwells on his tongue, and fills th' ethereal plain?
Enough—for ever cease your murm'ring breath;
Not as a foe, but friend converse with Death,
Since to the port of happiness unknown
He brought that treasure which you call your own.
The gift of heav'n intrusted to your hand
Cheerful resign at the divine command:
Not at your bar must sov'reign Wisdom stand.

AN HYMN TO HUMANITY

TO S. P. G. ESQ;

I

LO! for this dark terrestrial ball
Forsakes his azure-paved hall
  A prince of heav'nly birth!
Divine Humanity behold,
What wonders rise, what charms unfold
  At his descent to earth!

II

The bosoms of the great and good
With wonder and delight he view'd,
  And fix'd his empire there:
Him, close compressing to his breast,
The sire of gods and men address'd,
  "My son, my heav'nly fair!

III

"Descend to earth, there place thy throne;
"To succour man's afflicted son
  "Each human heart inspire:
"To act in bounties unconfin'd
"Enlarge the close contracted mind,
  "And fill it with thy fire."

IV

Quick as the word, with swift career
He wings his course from star to star,
  And leaves the bright abode.
The Virtue did his charms impart;
Their G——-! then thy raptur'd heart
  Perceiv'd the rushing God:

V

For when thy pitying eye did see
The languid muse in low degree,
  Then, then at thy desire
Descended the celestial nine;
O'er me methought they deign'd to shine,
  And deign'd to string my lyre.

VI

Can Afric's muse forgetful prove?
Or can such friendship fail to move
   A tender human heart?
Immortal Friendship laurel-crown'd
The smiling Graces all surround
   With ev'ry heav'nly Art.

TO THE
HONOURABLE T. H. ESQ;

ON THE DEATH OF HIS DAUGHTER

WHILE deep you mourn beneath the cypress-shade
The hand of Death, and your dear daughter laid
In dust, whose absence gives your tears to flow,
And racks your bosom with incessant woe,
Let Recollection take a tender part,
Assuage the raging tortures of your heart,
Still the wild tempest of tumultuous grief,
And pour the heav'nly nectar of relief:
Suspend the sigh, dear Sir, and check the groan,
Divinely bright your daughter's Virtues shone:
How free from scornful pride her gentle mind,
Which ne'er its aid to indigence declin'd!
Expanding free, it sought the means to prove
Unfailing charity, unbounded love!
    She unreluctant flies to see no more
Her dear-lov'd parents on earth's dusky shore:
Impatient heav'n's resplendent goal to gain,
She with swift progress cuts the azure plain,
Where grief subsides, where changes are no more,
And life's tumultuous billows cease to roar;
She leaves her earthly mansion for the skies,
Where new creations feast her wond'ring eyes.
    To heav'n's high mandate cheerfully resign'd
She mounts, and leaves the rolling globe behind;
She, who late wish'd that Leonard might return,

90

Has ceas'd to languish, and forgot to mourn;
To the same high empyreal mansions come,
She joins her spouse, and smiles upon the tomb:
And thus I hear her from the realms above:
"Lo! this the kingdom of celestial love!
"Could ye, fond parents, see our present bliss,
"How soon would you each sigh, each fear dismiss?
"Amidst unutter'd pleasures whilst I play
"In the fair sunshine of celestial day,
"As far as grief affects an happy soul
"So far doth grief my better mind controul,
"To see on earth my aged parents mourn,
"And secret wish for T—! to return:
"Let brighter scenes your ev'ning-hours employ:
"Converse with heav'n, and taste the promis'd joy"

NIOBE IN DISTRESS FOR HER CHILDREN SLAIN BY APOLLO

FROM OVID'S METAMORPHOSES, BOOK VI. AND FROM A VIEW OF THE PAINTING OF MR. RICHARD WILSON

APOLLO's wrath to man the dreadful spring
Of ills innum'rous, tuneful goddess, sing!
Thou who did'st first th' ideal pencil give,
And taught'st the painter in his works to live,
Inspire with glowing energy of thought,
What Wilson painted, and what Ovid wrote.
Muse! lend thy aid, nor let me sue in vain,
Tho' last and meanest of the rhyming train!
O guide my pen in lofty strains to show
The Phrygian queen, all beautiful in woe.
    'Twas where Maeonia spreads her wide domain
Niobe dwelt, and held her potent reign:
See in her hand the regal sceptre shine,
The wealthy heir of Tantalus divine,
He most distinguish'd by Dodonean Jove,
To approach the tables of the gods above:
Her grandsire Atlas, who with mighty pains
Th' ethereal axis on his neck sustains:
Her other grandsire on the throne on high
Rolls the loud-pealing thunder thro' the sky.
    Her spouse, Amphion, who from Jove too springs,
Divinely taught to sweep the sounding strings.
    Seven sprightly sons the royal bed adorn,

92

Seven daughters beauteous as the op'ning morn,
As when Aurora fills the ravish'd sight,
And decks the orient realms with rosy light
From their bright eyes the living splendors play,
Nor can beholders bear the flashing ray.
   Wherever, Niobe, thou turn'st thine eyes,
New beauties kindle, and new joys arise!
But thou had'st far the happier mother prov'd,
If this fair offspring had been less belov'd:
What if their charms exceed Aurora's teint.
No words could tell them, and no pencil paint,
Thy love too vehement hastens to destroy
Each blooming maid, and each celestial boy.
   Now Manto comes, endu'd with mighty skill,
The past to explore, the future to reveal.
Thro' Thebes' wide streets Tiresia's daughter came,
Divine Latona's mandate to proclaim:
The Theban maids to hear the orders ran,
When thus Maeonia's prophetess began:
   "Go, Thebans! great Latona's will obey,
"And pious tribute at her altars pay:
"With rights divine, the goddess be implor'd,
"Nor be her sacred offspring unador'd."
Thus Manto spoke. The Theban maids obey,
And pious tribute to the goddess pay.
The rich perfumes ascend in waving spires,
And altars blaze with consecrated fires;
The fair assembly moves with graceful air,
And leaves of laurel bind the flowing hair.
   Niobe comes with all her royal race,
With charms unnumber'd, and superior grace:
Her Phrygian garments of delightful hue,
Inwove with gold, refulgent to the view,
Beyond description beautiful she moves
Like heav'nly Venus, 'midst her smiles and loves:

She views around the supplicating train,
And shakes her graceful head with stern disdain,
Proudly she turns around her lofty eyes,
And thus reviles celestial deities:
"What madness drives the Theban ladies fair
"To give their incense to surrounding air?
"Say why this new sprung deity preferr'd?
"Why vainly fancy your petitions heard?
"Or say why Caeus offspring is obey'd,
"While to my goddesship no tribute's paid?
"For me no altars blaze with living fires,
"No bullock bleeds, no frankincense transpires,
"Tho' Cadmus' palace, not unknown to fame,
"And Phrygian nations all revere my name.
"Where'er I turn my eyes vast wealth I find,
"Lo! here an empress with a goddess join'd.
"What, shall a Titaness be deify'd,
"To whom the spacious earth a couch deny'd!
"Nor heav'n, nor earth, nor sea receiv'd your queen,
"Till pitying Delos took the wand'rer in.
"Round me what a large progeny is spread!
"No frowns of fortune has my soul to dread.
"What if indignant she decrease my train
"More than Latona's number will remain;
"Then hence, ye Theban dames, hence haste away,
"Nor longer off'rings to Latona pay;
"Regard the orders of Amphion's spouse,
"And take the leaves of laurel from your brows."
Niobe spoke. The Theban maids obey'd,
Their brows unbound, and left the rights unpaid.
    The angry goddess heard, then silence broke
On Cynthus' summit, and indignant spoke;
"Phoebus! behold, thy mother in disgrace,
"Who to no goddess yields the prior place
"Except to Juno's self, who reigns above,

"The spouse and sister of the thund'ring Jove.
"Niobe, sprung from Tantalus, inspires
"Each Theban bosom with rebellious fires;
"No reason her imperious temper quells,
"But all her father in her tongue rebels;
"Wrap her own sons for her blaspheming breath,
"Apollo! wrap them in the shades of death."
Latona ceas'd, and ardent thus replies
The God, whose glory decks th' expanded skies.
    "Cease thy complaints, mine be the task assign'd
"To punish pride, and scourge the rebel mind."
This Phoebe join'd.—They wing their instant flight;
Thebes trembled as th' immortal pow'rs alight.
    With clouds incompass'd glorious Phoebus stands;
The feather'd vengeance quiv'ring in his hands.
    Near Cadmus' walls a plain extended lay,
Where Thebes' young princes pass'd in sport the day:
There the bold coursers bounded o'er the plains,
While their great masters held the golden reins.
Ismenus first the racing pastime led,
And rul'd the fury of his flying steed.
"Ah me," he sudden cries, with shrieking breath,
While in his breast he feels the shaft of death;
He drops the bridle on his courser's mane,
Before his eyes in shadows swims the plain,
He, the first-born of great Amphion's bed,
Was struck the first, first mingled with the dead.
    Then didst thou, Sipylus, the language hear
Of fate portentous whistling in the air:
As when th' impending storm the sailor sees
He spreads his canvas to the fav'ring breeze,
So to thine horse thou gav'st the golden reins,
Gav'st him to rush impetuous o'er the plains:
But ah! a fatal shaft from Phoebus' hand
Smites thro' thy neck, and sinks thee on the sand.

Two other brothers were at wrestling found,
And in their pastime claspt each other round:
A shaft that instant from Apollo's hand
Transfixt them both, and stretcht them on the sand:
Together they their cruel fate bemoan'd,
Together languish'd, and together groan'd:
Together too th' unbodied spirits fled,
And sought the gloomy mansions of the dead.
Alphenor saw, and trembling at the view,
Beat his torn breast, that chang'd its snowy hue.
He flies to raise them in a kind embrace;
A brother's fondness triumphs in his face:
Alphenor fails in this fraternal deed,
A dart dispatch'd him (so the fates decreed:)
Soon as the arrow left the deadly wound,
His issuing entrails smoak'd upon the ground.
  What woes on blooming Damasichon wait!
His sighs portend his near impending fate.
Just where the well-made leg begins to be,
And the soft sinews form the supple knee,
The youth sore wounded by the Delian god
Attempts t' extract the crime-avenging rod,
But, whilst he strives the will of fate t' avert,
Divine Apollo sends a second dart;
Swift thro' his throat the feather'd mischief flies,
Bereft of sense, he drops his head, and dies.
  Young Ilioneus, the last, directs his pray'r,
And cries, "My life, ye gods celestial! spare."
Apollo heard, and pity touch'd his heart,
But ah! too late, for he had sent the dart:
Thou too, O Ilioneus, art doom'd to fall,
The fates refuse that arrow to recal.
  On the swift wings of ever flying Fame
To Cadmus' palace soon the tidings came:
Niobe heard, and with indignant eyes

96

She thus express'd her anger and surprise:
"Why is such privilege to them allow'd?
"Why thus insulted by the Delian god?
"Dwells there such mischief in the pow'rs above?
"Why sleeps the vengeance of immortal Jove?"
For now Amphion too, with grief oppress'd,
Had plung'd the deadly dagger in his breast.
Niobe now, less haughty than before,
With lofty head directs her steps no more
She, who late told her pedigree divine,
And drove the Thebans from Latona's shrine,
How strangely chang'd!—yet beautiful in woe,
She weeps, nor weeps unpity'd by the foe.
On each pale corse the wretched mother spread
Lay overwhelm'd with grief, and kiss'd her dead,
Then rais'd her arms, and thus, in accents slow,
"Be sated cruel Goddess! with my woe;
"If I've offended, let these streaming eyes,
"And let this sev'nfold funeral suffice:
"Ah! take this wretched life you deign'd to save,
"With them I too am carried to the grave.
"Rejoice triumphant, my victorious foe,
"But show the cause from whence your triumphs flow?
"Tho' I unhappy mourn these children slain,
"Yet greater numbers to my lot remain."
She ceas'd, the bow string twang'd with awful sound,
Which struck with terror all th' assembly round,
Except the queen, who stood unmov'd alone,
By her distresses more presumptuous grown.
Near the pale corses stood their sisters fair
In sable vestures and dishevell'd hair;
One, while she draws the fatal shaft away,
Faints, falls, and sickens at the light of day.
To sooth her mother, lo! another flies,
And blames the fury of inclement skies,

And, while her words a filial pity show,
Struck dumb—indignant seeks the shades below.
Now from the fatal place another flies,
Falls in her flight, and languishes, and dies.
Another on her sister drops in death;
A fifth in trembling terrors yields her breath;
While the sixth seeks some gloomy cave in vain,
Struck with the rest, and mingled with the slain.
   One only daughter lives, and she the least;
The queen close clasp'd the daughter to her breast:
"Ye heav'nly pow'rs, ah spare me one," she cry'd,
"Ah! spare me one," the vocal hills reply'd:
In vain she begs, the Fates her suit deny,
In her embrace she sees her daughter die.
   [4]"The queen of all her family bereft,
"Without or husband, son, or daughter left,
"Grew stupid at the shock. The passing air
"Made no impression on her stiff'ning hair.
"The blood forsook her face: amidst the flood
"Pour'd from her cheeks, quite fix'd her eye-balls stood.
"Her tongue, her palate both obdurate grew,
"Her curdled veins no longer motion knew;
"The use of neck, and arms, and feet was gone,
"And ev'n her bowels hard'ned into stone:
"A marble statue now the queen appears,
"But from the marble steal the silent tears."

---

4 This verse to the end is the work of another hand.

TO S. M.

A YOUNG AFRICAN PAINTER,
ON SEEING HIS WORKS

TO show the lab'ring bosom's deep intent,
And thought in living characters to paint,
When first thy pencil did those beauties give,
And breathing figures learnt from thee to live,
How did those prospects give my soul delight,
A new creation rushing on my sight?
Still, wond'rous youth! each noble path pursue,
On deathless glories fix thine ardent view:
Still may the painter's and the poet's fire
To aid thy pencil, and thy verse conspire!
And may the charms of each seraphic theme
Conduct thy footsteps to immortal fame!
High to the blissful wonders of the skies
Elate thy soul, and raise thy wishful eyes.
Thrice happy, when exalted to survey
That splendid city, crown'd with endless day,
Whose twice six gates on radiant hinges ring:
Celestial Salem blooms in endless spring.

Calm and serene thy moments glide along,
And may the muse inspire each future song!
Still, with the sweets of contemplation bless'd,
May peace with balmy wings your soul invest!
But when these shades of time are chas'd away,
And darkness ends in everlasting day,
On what seraphic pinions shall we move,

And view the landscapes in the realms above?
There shall thy tongue in heav'nly murmurs flow,
And there my muse with heav'nly transport glow:
No more to tell of Damon's tender sighs,
Or rising radiance of Aurora's eyes,
For nobler themes demand a nobler strain,
And purer language on th' ethereal plain.
Cease, gentle muse! the solemn gloom of night
Now seals the fair creation from my sight.

TO HIS HONOUR THE LIEUTENANT-GOVERNOR, ON THE DEATH OF HIS LADY

MARCH 24, 1773

ALL-Conquering Death! by thy resistless pow'r,
Hope's tow'ring plumage falls to rise no more!
Of scenes terrestrial how the glories fly,
Forget their splendors, and submit to die!
Who ere escap'd thee, but the saint[5] of old
Beyond the flood in sacred annals told,
And the great sage,[6] whom fiery coursers drew
To heav'n's bright portals from Elisha's view;
Wond'ring he gaz'd at the refulgent car,
Then snatch'd the mantle floating on the air.
From Death these only could exemption boast,
And without dying gain'd th' immortal coast.
Not falling millions sate the tyrant's mind,
Nor can the victor's progress be confin'd.
But cease thy strife with Death, fond Nature, cease:
He leads the virtuous to the realms of peace;
His to conduct to the immortal plains,
Where heav'n's Supreme in bliss and glory reigns.
　There sits, illustrious Sir, thy beauteous spouse;
A gem-blaz'd circle beaming on her brows.

5 Enoch.

6 Elijah.

Hail'd with acclaim among the heav'nly choirs,
Her soul new-kindling with seraphic fires,
To notes divine she tunes the vocal strings,
While heav'n's high concave with the music rings.
Virtue's rewards can mortal pencil paint?
No—all descriptive arts, and eloquence are faint;
Nor canst thou, Oliver, assent refuse
To heav'nly tidings from the Afric muse.

   As soon may change thy laws, eternal fate,
As the saint miss the glories I relate;
Or her Benevolence forgotten lie,
Which wip'd the trick'ling tear from Misry's eye.
Whene'er the adverse winds were known to blow,
When loss to loss ensu'd, and woe to woe,
Calm and serene beneath her father's hand
She sat resign'd to the divine command.

   No longer then, great Sir, her death deplore,
And let us hear the mournful sigh no more,
Restrain the sorrow streaming from thine eye,
Be all thy future moments crown'd with joy!
Nor let thy wishes be to earth confin'd,
But soaring high pursue th' unbodied mind.
Forgive the muse, forgive th' advent'rous lays,
That fain thy soul to heav'nly scenes would raise.

A FAREWEL
TO AMERICA

TO MRS. S. W.

I

ADIEU, New-England's smiling meads,
    Adieu, the flow'ry plain:
I leave thine op'ning charms, O spring,
    And tempt the roaring main.

II

In vain for me the flow'rets rise,
    And boast their gaudy pride,
While here beneath the northern skies
    I mourn for health deny'd.

III

Celestial maid of rosy hue,
    O let me feel thy reign!
I languish till thy face I view,
    Thy vanish'd joys regain.

IV

Susanna mourns, nor can I bear
  To see the crystal show'r,
Or mark the tender falling tear
  At sad departure's hour;

V

Not unregarding can I see
  Her soul with grief opprest:
But let no sighs, no groans for me,
  Steal from her pensive breast.

VI

In vain the feather'd warblers sing,
  In vain the garden blooms,
And on the bosom of the spring
  Breathes out her sweet perfumes.

VII

While for Britannia's distant shore
  We sweep the liquid plain,
And with astonish'd eyes explore
  The wide-extended main.

VIII

Lo! Health appears! celestial dame!
  Complacent and serene,
With Hebe's mantle o'er her Frame,
  With soul-delighting mein.

IX

To mark the vale where London lies
  With misty vapours crown'd,
Which cloud Aurora's thousand dyes,
  And veil her charms around.

X

Why, Phoebus, moves thy car so slow?
  So slow thy rising ray?
Give us the famous town to view,
  Thou glorious king of day!

XI

For thee, Britannia, I resign
  New-England's smiling fields;
To view again her charms divine,
  What joy the prospect yields!

XII

But thou! Temptation hence away,
  With all thy fatal train,
Nor once seduce my soul away,
  By thine enchanting strain.

XIII

Thrice happy they, whose heav'nly shield
  Secures their souls from harms,
And fell Temptation on the field
  Of all its pow'r disarms!

Boston, May 7, 1773.

A REBUS

BY I. B.

I

A BIRD delicious to the taste,
On which an army once did feast,
  Sent by an hand unseen;
A creature of the horned race,
Which Britain's royal standards grace;
  A gem of vivid green;

II

A town of gaiety and sport,
Where beaux and beauteous nymphs resort,
  And gallantry doth reign;
A Dardan hero fam'd of old
For youth and beauty, as we're told,
  And by a monarch slain;

III

A peer of popular applause,
Who doth our violated laws,
   And grievances proclaim.
Th' initials show a vanquish'd town,
That adds fresh glory and renown
   To old Britannia's fame.

AN ANSWER
TO THE REBUS

BY THE AUTHOR OF THESE POEMS

THE poet asks, and Phillis can't refuse
To show th' obedience of the Infant muse.
She knows the Quail of most inviting taste
Fed Israel's army in the dreary waste;
And what's on Britain's royal standard borne,
But the tall, graceful, rampant Unicorn?
The Emerald with a vivid verdure glows
Among the gems which regal crowns compose;
Boston's a town, polite and debonair,
To which the beaux and beauteous nymphs repair,
Each Helen strikes the mind with sweet surprise,
While living lightning flashes from her eyes,
See young Euphorbus of the Dardan line
By Manelaus' hand to death resign:
The well known peer of popular applause
Is C—m zealous to support our laws.
Quebec now vanquish'd must obey,
She too much annual tribute pay
To Britain of immortal fame.
And add new glory to her name.

AN ADDRESS
TO THE ATHEIST

Muse! where shall I begin the spacious feild
To tell what curses unbeleif doth yeild?
Thou who dost daily feel his hand, and rod
Darest thou deny the Essence of a God! —
If there's no heav'n, ah! whither wilt thou go
Make thy Ilysium in the shades below?
If there's no God from whom did all things Spring
He made the greatest and minutest Thing
Angelic ranks no less his Power display
Than the least mite scarce visible to Day
With vast astonishment my soul is struck
Have Reason'g powers thy darken'd breast forsook?
The Laws deep Graven by the hand of God,
Seal'd with Immanuel's all-redeeming blood:
This second point thy folly dares deny
On thy devoted head for vengeance cry —
Turn then I pray thee from the dangerous road
Rise from the dust and seek the mighty God.
His is bright truth without a dark disguise
And his are wisdom's all beholding Eyes:
With labour'd snares our Adversary great
Withholds from us the Kingdom and the seat.
Bliss weeping waits thee, in her Arms to fly
To her own regions of felicity —
Perhaps thy ignorance will ask us where?
Go to the Corner stone he will declare.
Thy heart in unbelief will harden'd grow

110

Tho' much indulg'd in vicious pleasure now —
Thou tak'st unusual means; the path forbear
Unkind to others to thy self Severe —
Methinks I see the consequence thou'rt blind
Thy unbelief disturbs the peaceful Mind.
The endless scene too far for me to tread
Too great to utter from so weak a head.
That man his maker's love divine might know
In heavens high firmament he placed his Bow
To shew his covenant for ever sure
To endless Age unchanging to endure —
He made the Heavens and earth that lasting Spring
Of admiration! To whom dost thou bring
Thy grateful tribute? Adoration pay
To heathen Gods? Can wise Apollo say
Tis I that saves thee from the deepest hell;
Minerva teach thee all thy days to tell?
Doth Pluto tell thee thou Shalt see the shade
Of fell perdition for transgression made?
Doth Cupid in thy breast that warmth inspire
To love thy Brother, which is God's desire?
Atheist! behold the wide extended skies
And wisdom infinite shall strike thine eyes
Mark rising Sol when far he spreads his Ray
And his Commission read — To rule the Day
At night behold that silver Regent bright
And her command to lead the train of Night
Lo! how the Stars all vocal in his praise
Witness his Essence in celestial lays!

AN ADDRESS
TO THE DEIST

Must Ethiopians be employ'd for you?
Much I rejoice if any good I do.
I ask O unbeleiver, Satan's child
Hath not thy Saviour been too much revil'd
Th' auspicious rays that round his temples shine
Do still declare him to be Christ divine
Doth not the great Eternal call him Son
Is he not pleas'd with his beloved One —
How canst thou thus divide the Trinity —
The blest the Holy the eternal three
Tis Satan's Snares are fluttering in the wind
Whereby he doth insnare thy foolish mind
God, the Eternal Orders this to be
Sees thy vain arg'ments to divide the three
Cans't thou not see the Consequence in store?
Begin th' Almighty monarch to adore
Attend to Reason whispering in thine ear
Seek the Eternal while he is so near.
Full in thy view I point each path I know
Lest to the vale of black dispair I go.
At the last day where wilt thou hide thy face
That Day approaching is no time for Grace.
Too late perceive thyself undone and lost
To late own Father, Son, and Holy Ghost.
Who trod the wine-press of Jehovah's wrath?
Who taught us prayer, and promis'd grace and faith?
Who but the Son, who reigns supremely blest

Ever, and ever, in immortal rest.?
The vilest prodigal who comes to God
Is not cast out but bro't by Jesus' blood.
When to the faithless Jews he oft did cry
Some own'd this teacher Some made him a lye
He came to you in mean apparel clad
He came to Save us from our Sins, and had
Compassion more than language can express.
Pains his companions, and his friends distress
Immanuel on the cross those pains did bear —
Will the eternal our petitions hear?
Ah! wondrous Distiny his life he laid.
"Father forgive them," thus the Saviour pray'd
Nail'd was King Jesus on the cross for us.
For our transgressions he sustain'd the Curse.

ON MESSRS
HUSSEY AND COFFIN

Did Fear and Danger so perplex your Mind,
As made you fearful of the Whistling Wind?
Was it not Boreas knit his angry Brow
Against you? or did Consideration bow?
To lend you Aid, did not his Winds combine?
To stop your passage with a churlish Line,
Did haughty Eolus with Contempt look down
With Aspect windy, and a study'd Frown?
Regard them not; — the Great Supreme, the Wise,
Intends for something hidden from our Eyes.
Suppose the groundless Gulph had snatch'd away
Hussey and Coffin to the raging Sea;
Where wou'd they go? where wou'd be their Abode?
With the supreme and independent God,
Or made their Beds down in the Shades below,
Where neither Pleasure nor Content can flow.
To Heaven their Souls with eager Raptures soar,
Enjoy the Bliss of him they wou'd adore.
Had the soft gliding Streams of Grace been near,
Some favourite Hope their fainting hearts to cheer,
Doubtless the Fear of Danger far had fled:
No more repeated Victory crown their Heads.

TO THE HONBLE
COMMODORE HOOD

ON HIS PARDONING A DESERTER

It was thy noble soul and high desert
That caus'd these breathings of my grateful heart
You sav'd a soul from Pluto's dreary shore
You sav'd his body and he asks no more
This generous act Immortal wreaths shall bring
To thee for meritorious was the Spring
From whence from whence, [sic] this candid ardor flow'd
To grace thy name, and Glorify thy God
The Eatherial spirits in the realms above
Rejoice to see thee exercise thy Love
Hail: Commodore may heaven delighted pour
Its blessings plentious in a silent shower
The voice of pardon did resound on high
While heaven consented, and he must not die
On thee, fair victor be the Blessing shed
And rest for ever on thy matchless Head.

ON FRIENDSHIP

Let amicitia in her ample reign
Extend her notes to a Celestial strain
Benevolent far more divinely Bright
Amor like me doth triumph at the sight
When my thoughts in gratitude imploy
Mental Imaginations give me Joy
Now let my thoughts in Contemplation steer
The Footsteps of the Superlative fair

Boston, July 15, 1769

ON THE
DEATH OF MR. SNIDER

MURDER'D BY RICHARDSON

In heavens eternal court it was decreed
Thou the first martyr for the common good
Long hid before, a vile infernal here
Prevents Achilles in his mid career
Where'er this fury darts his Pois'nous breath
All are endanger'd to the shafts of death
The generous Sires beheld the fatal wound
Saw their young champion gasping on the ground
They rais'd him up but to each present ear
What martial glories did his tongue declare
The wretch appal'd no longer can despise
But from the Striking victim turns his eyes--
When this young martial genius did appear
The Tory chief no longer could forbear.
Ripe for destruction, see the wretches doom
He waits the curses of the age to come
In vain he flies, by Justice Swiftly chaced
With unexpected infamy disgraced
By Richardson for ever banish'd here
The grand Usurpers bravely vaunted Heir.
We bring the body from the watry bower
To lodge it where it shall remove no more
Snider behold with what Majestic Love
The Illustrious retinue begins to move

With Secret rage fair freedom's foes beneath
See in thy corse ev'n Majesty in Death.

OCEAN

Now muse divine, thy heav'nly aid impart,
The feast of Genius, and the play of Art.
From high Parnassus' radiant top repair,
Celestial Nine! propitious to my pray'r.
In vain my Eyes explore the wat'ry reign,
By you unaided with the flowing strain.
When first old Chaos of tyrannic soul
Wav'd his dread Sceptre o'er the boundless whole,
Confusion reign'd till the divine Command
On floating azure fix'd the Solid Land,
Till first he call'd the latent seeds of light,
And gave dominion o'er eternal Night.
From deepest glooms he rais'd this ample Ball,
And round its walls he bade its surges roll;
With instant haste the new made seas complyd,
And the globe rolls impervious to the Tide;
Yet when the mighty Sire of Ocean frownd
"His awful trident shook the solid Ground."
The King of Tempests thunders o'er the plain,
And scorns the azure monarch of the main,
He sweeps the surface, makes the billows rore,
And furious, lash the loud resounding shore.
His pinion'd race his dread commands obey,
Syb's, Eurus, Boreas, drive the foaming sea!
See the whole stormy progeny descend!
And waves on waves devolving without End,
But cease Eolus, all thy winds restrain,
And let us view the wonders of the main
Where the proud Courser paws the blue abode,

Impetuous bounds, and mocks the driver's rod.
There, too, the Heifer fair as that which bore
Divine Europa to the Cretan shore.
With guileless mein the gentle Creature strays,
Quaffs the pure stream, and crops ambrosial Grass.
Again with recent wonder I survey
The finny sov'reign bask in hideous play.
(So fancy sees) he makes a tempest rise
And intercept the azure vaulted skies.
Such is his sport:—but if his anger glow
What kindling vengeance boils the deep below!
Twas but e'er now an Eagle young and gay
Pursu'd his passage thro' the aierial way.
He aim'd his piece, would Calef's hand do more ?
Yes, him he brought to pluto's dreary shore.
Slow breathed his last, the painful minutes move
With lingring pace his rashness to reprove;
Perhaps his father's Just commands he bore
To fix dominion on some distant shore.
Ah! me unblest he cries. Oh! had I staid
Or swift my Father's mandate had obey'd.
But ah! too late.—Old Ocean heard his cries.
He stroakes his hoary tresses and replies:
What mean these plaints so near our wat'ry throne,
And what the Cause of this distressful moan?
Confess, Iscarius, let thy words be true
Not let me find a faithless Bird in you.
His voice struck terror thro' the whole domain.
Aw'd by his frowns the royal youth began,
Saw you not, Sire, a tall and Gallant ship
Which proudly skims the surface of the deep?
With pompous form from Boston's port she came,
She flies, and London her resounding name.
O'er the rough surge the dauntless Chief prevails
For partial Aura fills his swelling sails.

His fatal musket shortens thus my day
And thus the victor takes my life away.
Faint with his wound Iscarius said no more,
His Spirit sought Oblivion's sable shore.
This Neptune saw, and with a hollow groan
Resum'd the azure honours of his Throne.

TO A
GENTLEMAN OF THE NAVY

Celestial muse! for sweetness fam'd inspire
My wondrous theme with true poetic fire,
Rochfort, for thee! And Greaves deserve my lays
The sacred tribute of ingenuous praise.
For here, true merit shuns the glare of light,
She loves oblivion, and evades the sight.
At sight of her, see dawning genius rise
And stretch her pinions to her native skies.
Paris, for Helen's bright resistless charms,
Made Illion bleed and set the world in arms,
Had you appear'd on the Achaian shore
Troy now had stood, and Helen charm'd no more.
The Phrygian hero had resign'd the dame
For purer joys in friendship's sacred flame,
The noblest gift, and of immortal kind,
That brightens, dignifies the manly mind.
Calliope, half gracious to my prayer,
Grants but the half and scatters half in air.
Far in the space where ancient Albion keeps
Amidst the roarings of the sacred deeps,
Where willing forests leave their native plain,
Descend, and instant, plough the wat'ry main.
Strange to relate! with canvas wings they speed
To distant worlds; of distant worlds the dread.
The trembling natives of the peaceful plain,
Astonish'd view the heroes of the main,
Wond'ring to see two chiefs of matchless grace,

Of generous bosom, and ingenuous face,
From ocean sprung, like ocean foes to rest,
The thirst of glory burns each youthful breast.
In virtue's cause, the muse implores for grace,
These blooming sons of Neptune's royal race;
Cerulean youths! your joint assent declare,
Virtue to rev'rence, more than mortal fair,
A crown of glory, which the muse will twine,
Immortal trophy! Rochfort shall be thine!
Thine too O Greaves! for virtue's offspring share,
Celestial friendship and the muse's care.
Yours is the song, and your's the honest praise,
Lo! Rochfort smiles, and Greaves approves my lays.

HIS EXCELLENCY
GENERAL WASHINGTON

Celestial choir! enthron'd in realms of light,
Columbia's scenes of glorious toils I write.
While freedom's cause her anxious breast alarms,
She flashes dreadful in refulgent arms.
See mother earth her offspring's fate bemoan,
And nations gaze at scenes before unknown!
See the bright beams of heaven's revolving light
Involved in sorrows and the veil of night!
The Goddess comes, she moves divinely fair,
Olive and laurel binds Her golden hair:
Wherever shines this native of the skies,
Unnumber'd charms and recent graces rise.
Muse! Bow propitious while my pen relates
How pour her armies through a thousand gates,
As when Eolus heaven's fair face deforms,
Enwrapp'd in tempest and a night of storms;
Astonish'd ocean feels the wild uproar,
The refluent surges beat the sounding shore;
Or think as leaves in Autumn's golden reign,
Such, and so many, moves the warrior's train.
In bright array they seek the work of war,
Where high unfurl'd the ensign waves in air.
Shall I to Washington their praise recite?
Enough thou know'st them in the fields of fight.
Thee, first in peace and honors—we demand
The grace and glory of thy martial band.
Fam'd for thy valour, for thy virtues more,

124

Hear every tongue thy guardian aid implore!
   One century scarce perform'd its destined round,
When Gallic powers Columbia's fury found;
And so may you, whoever dares disgrace
The land of freedom's heaven-defended race!
Fix'd are the eyes of nations on the scales,
For in their hopes Columbia's arm prevails.
Anon Britannia droops the pensive head,
While round increase the rising hills of dead.
Ah! Cruel blindness to Columbia's state!
Lament thy thirst of boundless power too late.
   Proceed, great chief, with virtue on thy side,
Thy ev'ry action let the Goddess guide.
A crown, a mansion, and a throne that shine,
With gold unfading, WASHINGTON! Be thine.

ON THE
CAPTURE OF GENERAL LEE

The deed perfidious, and the Hero's fate,
In tender strains, celestial Muse! relate.
The latent foe to friendship makes pretence
The name assumes without the sacred sense!
He, with a rapture well dissembl'd, press'd
The hero's hand, and fraudful, thus address'd.
"O friend belov'd! may heaven its aid afford,
And spread yon troops beneath thy conquering sword!
Grant to America's united prayer
A glorious conquest on the field of war.
But thou indulgent to my warm request
Vouchsafe thy presence as my honour'd guest:
From martial cares a space unbend thy soul
In social banquet, and the sprightly bowl."
Thus spoke the foe; and warlike Lee reply'd,
"Ill fits it me, who such an army guide;
To whom his conduct each brave soldier owes
To waste an hour in banquets or repose:
This day important, with loud voice demands
Our wisest Counsels, and our bravest hands."
Thus having said he heav'd a boding sigh.
The hour approach'd that damps Columbia's Joy.
Inform'd, conducted, by the treach'rous friend
With winged speed the adverse train attend
Ascend the Dome, and seize with frantic air
The self surrender'd glorious prize of war!
On sixty coursers, swifter than the wind

They fly, and reach the British camp assign'd.
Arriv'd, what transport touch'd their leader's breast!
Who thus deriding, the brave Chief address'd.
"Say, art thou he, beneath whose vengeful hands
Our best of heroes grasp'd in death the sands?
One fierce regard of thine indignant eye
Turn'd Brittain pale, and made her armies fly;
But Oh! how chang'd! a prisoner in our arms
Till martial honour, dreadful in her charms,
Shall grace Britannia at her sons' return,
And widow'd thousands in our triumphs mourn."
While thus he spoke, the hero of renown
Survey'd the boaster with a gloomy frown
And stern reply'd. " Oh arrogance of tongue!
And wild ambition, ever prone to wrong!
Believ'st thou Chief, that armies such as thine
Can stretch in dust that heaven-defended line?
In vain allies may swarm from distant lands
And demons aid in formidable bands.
Great as thou art, thou shun'st the field of fame
Disgrace to Brittain, and the British name!
When offer'd combat by the noble foe,
(Foe to mis-rule), why did thy sword forgo
The easy conquest of the rebel-land?
Perhaps too easy for thy martial hand.
What various causes to the field invite!
For plunder you , and we for freedom fight:
Her cause divine with generous ardor fires,
And every bosom glows as she inspires!
Already, thousands of your troops are fled
To the drear mansions of the silent dead:
Columbia too, beholds with streaming eyes
Her heroes fall — 'tis freedom's sacrifice!
So wills the Power who with convulsive storms
Shakes impious realms, and nature's face deforms.

Yet those brave troops innum'rous as the sands
One soul inspires, one General Chief commands
Find in your train of boasted heroes, one
To match the praise of Godlike Washington.
Thrice happy Chief! in whom the virtues join,
And heaven-taught prudence speaks the man divine!"
He ceas'd. Amazement struck the warrior-train,
And doubt of conquest, on the hostile plain.

TO MR. AND MRS.—

ON THE DEATH OF THEIR INFANT SON

O DEATH! whose sceptre, trembling realms obey,
And weeping millions mourn thy savage sway;
Say, shall we call thee by the name of friend,
Who blasts our joys, and bids our glories end?
Behold, a child who rivals op'ning morn,
When its first beams the eastern hills adorn;
So sweetly blooming once that lovely boy,
His father's hope, his mother's only joy,
Nor charms nor innocence prevail to save,
From the grim monarch of the gloomy grave!
Two moons revolve when lo! among the dead
The beauteous infant lays his weary head:
For long he strove the tyrant to withstand,
And the dread terrors of his iron hand;
Vain was his strife, with the relentless power,
His efforts weak; and this his mortal hour;
He sinks—he dies—celestial muse, relate,
His spirit's entrance at the sacred gate.
Methinks I hear the heav'nly courts resound,
The recent theme inspires the choirs around.
His guardian angel with delight unknown,
Hails his bless'd charge on his immortal throne;
His heart expands at scenes unknown before,
Dominions praise, and prostate thrones adore;
Before the Eternal's feet their crowns are laid,

The glowing seraph vails his sacred head.
Spirits redeem'd, that more than angels shine,
For nobler praises tune their harps divine:
These saw his entrance; his soft hand they press'd,
Sat on his throne, and smiling thus address'd,
"Hail: thou! thrice welcome to this happy shore,
Born to new life where changes are no more;
Glad heaven receives thee, and thy God bestows,
Immortal youth exempt from pain and woes.
Sorrow and sin, those foes to human rest,
Forever banish'd from thy happy breast."
Gazing they spoke, and raptur'd thus replies,
The beauteous stranger in the etherial skies.
"Thus safe conducted to your bless'd abodes,
With sweet surprize I mix among the Gods;
The vast profound of this amazing grace,
Beyond your search, immortal powers, I praise;
Great Sire, I sing thy boundless love divine,
Mine is the bliss, but all the glory thine."
All heav'n rejoices as your . . . sings,
To heavenly airs he tunes the sounding strings;
Mean time on earth the hapless parents mourn,
"Too quickly fled, ah! never to return."
Thee, the vain visions of the night restore,
Illusive fancy paints the phantom o'er;
Fain would we clasp him, but he wings his flight;
Deceives our arms, and mixes with the night;
But oh! suppress the clouds of grief that roll,
Invading peace, and dark'ning all the soul.
Should heaven restore him to your arms again,
Oppress'd with woes, a painful endless train,
How would your prayers, your ardent wishes, rise,
Safe to repose him in his native skies.

AN ELEGY ON LEAVING

FAREWEL! ye friendly bow'rs, ye streams adieu,
I leave with sorrow each sequester'd seat:
The lawns, where oft I swept the morning dew,
The groves, from noon-tide rays a kind retreat.
Yon wood-crown'd hill, whose far projecting shade,
Inverted trembles in the limpid lake:
Where wrapt in thought I pensively have stray'd,
For crowds and noise, reluctant, I forsake.
The solemn pines, that, winding through the vale.
In graceful rows attract the wand'ring eye,
Where the soft ring-dove pours her soothing tale,
No more must veil me from the fervid sky.
Beneath yon aged oak's protecting arms,
Oft-times beside the pebbl'd brook I lay;
Where, pleas'd with simple Nature's various charms,
I pass'd in grateful solitude the day.
Rapt with the melody of Cynthio's strain,
There first my bosom felt poetic flame;
Mute was the bleating language of the plain,
And with his lays the wanton fawns grew tame.
But, ah! those pleasing hours are ever flown;
Ye scenes of transport from my thoughts retire;
Those rural joys no more the day shall crown,
No more my hand shall wake the warbling lyre.
But come, sweet Hope, from thy divine retreat,
Come to my breast, and chase my cares away,
Bring calm Content to gild my gloomy seat,
And cheer my bosom with her heav'nly ray.

131

Made in the USA
Las Vegas, NV
04 April 2022

46826494R00080